Pro .NET 5 Custom Libraries

Implementing Custom .NET Data Types

Roger Villela

Apress®

Pro .NET 5 Custom Libraries: Implementing Custom .NET Data Types

Roger Villela
Sao Paulo, São Paulo, Brazil

ISBN-13 (pbk): 978-1-4842-6390-7   ISBN-13 (electronic): 978-1-4842-6391-4
https://doi.org/10.1007/978-1-4842-6391-4

Managing Director, Apress Media LLC: Welmoed Spahr
Acquisitions Editor: Smriti Srivastava
Development Editor: Matthew Moodie
Coordinating Editor: Shrikant Vishwakarma

Cover designed by eStudioCalamar

Cover image designed by Pexels

Distributed to the book trade worldwide by Springer Science+Business Media LLC, 1 New York Plaza, Suite 4600, New York, NY 10004. Phone 1-800-SPRINGER, fax (201) 348-4505, email orders-ny@springer-sbm. com, or visit www.springeronline.com. Apress Media, LLC is a California LLC, and the sole member (owner) is Springer Science + Business Media Finance Inc (SSBM Finance Inc). SSBM Finance Inc is a **Delaware** corporation.

For information on translations, please e-mail booktranslations@springernature.com; for reprint, paperback, or audio rights, please e-mail bookpermissions@springernature.com.

Apress titles may be purchased in bulk for academic, corporate, or promotional use. eBook versions and licenses are also available for most titles. For more information, reference our Print and eBook Bulk Sales web page at www.apress.com/bulk-sales.

Any source code or other supplementary material referenced by the author in this book is available to readers on GitHub via the book's product page, located at www.apress.com/978-1-4842-6390-7. For more detailed information, please visit www.apress.com/source-code.

Printed on acid-free paper

This book is dedicated to my mother, Marina Roel de Oliveira.

January 14, 1952 to March 17, 2017 (†)

Table of Contents

About the Author vii

About the Technical Reviewer ix

Acknowledgments xi

Introduction xiii

Chapter 1: .NET Platform 1

Acronyms 1

ECMA-335 and .NET 2

ECMA-335 2

.NET Platform 8

About the Common Type System 13

Fundamental Types and Hardware Platform 13

The Organization of Fundamental Data Types 14

CTS for Fundamental Types 16

Virtual Execution System 18

.NET Module 19

.NET Assemblies 20

Chapter 2: Custom .NET Data Type 29

Management of Data Types 29

Working with System.Object, the Root of .NET Reference Types 29

System.ValueType, the Root of .NET Value Types 35

Methods 38

Chapter 3: .NET Methods: Implementation Details 51

Methods 51

About the Use of Operators 51

Operator Overloading: Programming Language Semantics and Syntaxes 54

Working with System.Object.GetType() 57

Constructors in a .NET Data Type 59

Chapter 4: .NET Special Members: Constructors in a Managed Environment 63

Acronyms 63

Special Members 63

About Constructors in a Managed Execution Environment 64

Default Constructor 64

Summary 73

Chapter 5: Finalizer Method: The .NET Special Member 75

Special Members 75

Special Member Destructor 75

Special Member Finalizer Method (Destructor) 82

Chapter 6: .NET Manifest and Versioning for Managed Libraries 89

Assemblies, Modules, Manifest, Versioning 89

Assembly 90

Manifest 90

Module 93

Versioning 95

Chapter 7: .NET Assemblies in a Managed Execution Environment 97

Managed Libraries 97

Data Types, Components, and Functionalities 98

Native Code and Managed Code 102

Index 113

About the Author

Roger Villela is a software engineer and entrepreneur with almost 30 years of experience in the industry and works as an independent professional. Currently, he is focused on his work as a book author and technical educator and specializes in the inner workings of orthogonal features of the following Microsoft development platforms and specialized application programming interfaces (APIs):

- Microsoft Windows operating system base services

- Microsoft Windows APIs architecture and engineering

- Microsoft Universal Windows Platform (UWP)

- Microsoft WinRT platform

- Microsoft .NET Framework implementation of the runtime environment (Common Language Runtime [CLR])

His work is based on Microsoft Windows software development kit (SDK) tools and libraries, Microsoft Visual Studio, and platform foundational APIs, architectures, and engineering. He works with the Microsoft Windows operating system, incorporating the following programming languages, extensions, and projections:

- C/C++

- Assembly (Intel IA-32/Intel 64 [x64/amd64])

- Component extensions/projections for runtimes

- C++/CLI

- C++/CX

- C++/WinRT

- C#

- Common Intermediate Language (Microsoft Intermediate Language [MSIL]) implementation for CLR platforms

About the Technical Reviewer

 **Carsten Thomsen** is a back-end developer primarily, but he works with smaller front-end bits as well. He has authored and reviewed a number of books, and created numerous Microsoft Learning courses, all to do with software development. He works as a freelancer/contractor in various countries in Europe, using Azure, Visual Studio, Azure DevOps, and GitHub as some of his tools. He is an exceptional troubleshooter, asking the right questions, including the less-logical ones (in a most-logical to least-logical fashion). He also enjoys working with architecture, research, analysis, development, testing, and bug fixing. Carsten is a very good communicator with great mentoring and team-lead skills, and he also excels at researching and presenting new material.

Acknowledgments

I want to thank to the Apress team who worked with me on this book: Smriti Srivastava (Acquisitions Editor), Shrikant Vishwakarma (Coordinating Editor), Matthew Moodie (Development Editor), Welmoed Spahr (Managing Director), and Carsten Thomsen (Technical Reviewer). It was a pleasure and an honor to work with such a highly professional team.

I also want to thank my parents, with a special nod to my dad (Gilberto), my two brothers (Eder and Marlos and his wife Janaína), my nephew Gabriel, my nieces Lívia and Rafaela, and my cousin Ariadne Villela.

I must also express special thanks to my friends Paula Carolina Damasio, Alessandro Augusto de Jesus, and Neide Pimenta. I also want to acknowledge and thank all the people who work really hard on team Praxio Tecnologia developing one of the greatest specialized enterprise resource planning (ERP) products on the market; congratulations to all of you for your efforts.

I also want to thank my professional colleagues and friends who have worked with me throughout the years.

Introduction

This book covers programming with .NET 5 to develop custom data types and custom libraries for use on Microsoft Windows, Linux, and Apple macOS. These custom libraries can be used in different operating system platforms because they are written using .NET 5 (a cross-platform implementation of the ECMA-335 specification) and because all source code is written in the C# programming language and uses only cross-platform Base Class Library (BCL) types.

This book focuses on how to best exploit the .NET 5 custom data types for software libraries so that companies and software engineers can design and implement internal/commercial tools for various scenarios on myriad target platforms. Contextual modeling and planning is difficult without a fundamental understanding of the .NET 5 platform, which this book seeks to provide. The book also covers internal aspects of the BCL .NET types and APIs, with walkthroughs covering the implementation process of custom .NET data types and .NET custom libraries.

You will also learn about .NET assembly and .NET module structures, the inner workings of the BCL implementation on the .NET platform, custom data types available through the .NET platform, and how to write a custom library that incorporates .NET APIs available through the .NET BCL.

CHAPTER 1

.NET Platform

This chapter provides an overview of .NET 5 (previously .NET Core) and describes the fundamental architectural and the engineering features that you should expect in any implementation of .NET 5 (regardless of hardware, operating system, or execution system).

Acronyms

The following acronyms are introduced in this chapter:

- Base Class Library (BCL)

- Common Intermediate Language (CIL)

- Common Language Infrastructure (CLI)

- Common Language Runtime (CLR)

- Common Type System (CTS)

- Framework Class Library (FCL) (Although not specific to the .NET Framework implementation, the term is used for the full range of .NET types available in an official distribution of .NET.)

- Intermediate Language (IL)

- Microsoft Intermediate Language (MSIL)

- Virtual Execution System (VES)

- Windows Presentation Foundation (WPF) (a.k.a. *execution engine*)

© Roger Villela 2020
R. Villela, *Pro .NET 5 Custom Libraries*, https://doi.org/10.1007/978-1-4842-6391-4_1

ECMA-335 and .NET

ECMA-335

The ECMA-335 standard specification defines the Common Language Infrastructure (CLI), which includes a set of conceptual definitions and rules to be followed and engineering mechanisms to be implemented, independent of the target operating system and hardware platforms. The CLI ensures that applications, components, and libraries can be written in multiple high-level languages and can be executed in different target system environments without needing to be rewritten.

We can access the ECMA-335 specification at www.ecma-international.org/publications/standards/Ecma-335.htm. Figure 1-1 shows an excerpt. The download link is www.ecma-international.org/publications/files/ECMA-ST/ECMA-335.pdf, and the XML specification download link is www.ecma-international.org/publications/files/ECMA-ST/ECMA-335.zip.

This Standard defines the Common Language Infrastructure (CLI) in which applications written in multiple high-level languages can be executed in different system environments without the need to rewrite those applications to take into consideration the unique characteristics of those environments. This Standard consists of the following parts:

- Partition I: Concepts and Architecture – Describes the overall architecture of the CLI, and provides the normative description of the Common Type System (CTS), the Virtual Execution System (VES), and the Common Language Specification (CLS). It also provides an informative description of the metadata.
- Partition II: Metadata Definition and Semantics – Provides the normative description of the metadata: its physical layout (as a file format), its logical contents (as a set of tables and their relationships), and its semantics (as seen from a hypothetical assembler, *ilasm*).
- Partition III: CIL Instruction Set – Describes the Common Intermediate Language (CIL) instruction set.
- Partition IV: Profiles and Libraries – Provides an overview of the CLI Libraries, and a specification of their factoring into Profiles and Libraries. A companion file, CLILibrary.xml, considered to be part of this Partition, but distributed in XML format, provides details of each class, value type, and interface in the CLI Libraries.
- Partition V: Debug Interchange Format – Describes a standard way to interchange debugging information between CLI producers and consumers.
- Partition VI: Annexes – Contains some sample programs written in CIL Assembly Language (ILAsm), information about a particular implementation of an assembler, a machine-readable description of the CIL instruction set which can be used to derive parts of the grammar used by this assembler as well as other tools that manipulate CIL, a set of guidelines used in the design of the libraries of Partition IV, and portability considerations.

Figure 1-1. *Excerpt of web page with information about the ECMA-335 standard specification*

More objectively, the CLI is an open specification that describes executable code and an execution environment that enables multiple high-level languages to be used on different architectural platforms without being rewritten.

This execution environment must follow the architectural infrastructure described by the following:

- *Base Class Library (BCL)*: Foundational library defined by and part of the CLI standard specification. It is implemented by .NET Framework, .NET Core, .NET 5, and .NET 6 (early stages, available on Github.com), and is the main reason for the existence of the .NET standard.

- *Common Language Specification (CLS)*: Rules (restrictions and models) required for language interoperability. The detailed information on the CLS group is a subset of what is in the CTS, but the content is primarily for language designers and class library designers (frameworks). So, learning about CTS will offer a great base of knowledge for you and your team for when we start working with the rules in the CLS.

- *Common Type System (CTS)*: The CTS is a set of data types and operations that are shared by all languages that support the CTS, and learning about the CTS will offer a great base of knowledge to you and your team when we start working with the rules in the CLS.

- *Metadata*: The metadata describes the program structure, enabling languages and tools to work together. Detailed understanding of the metadata group is not a requisite for a component developer or application developer. Instead, detailed information about such is primarily for tool builders and compiler writers.

- *Virtual Execution Engine (VES)*: How code is executed (and how types are instantiated), interacts, and dies. More abstractly, it is also known as an execution engine or execution environment. This execution system is responsible for loading, instantiating, executing, and ensuring the cohesiveness of the interactions between the instances. In brief, it offers entire lifecycle support for the instance of the types. The execution engine understands concepts, architecture, and implementation details of two fundamental areas of the platform: the CTS and the VES.

- *Semantics*:

  - Capability to recognize contextuality (semantics), meaning mechanisms to constantly observe your own environment and ways to guarantee advanced security rules, data integrity (acting based on more flexible or disciplined rules), dynamic extensibility and expandability. In addition, we have the capability to interact with highly specialized environments (advanced data management systems, for example), development software environment systems (for instance, Microsoft Visual Studio), different target operating systems and hardware platforms (for example, the Microsoft Windows operating system implementations and UNIX-based operating system implementations, including Linux distributions, Apple MacOS, Apple iOS, Google Android, FreeBSD, IBM AIX, Red Hat Linux, Intel x86/Intel x64, ARM 32-bit, ARM 64-bit, IoT high-specialized environment for embedded systems, web development, desktop development, mobile development, game development, artificial intelligence development, machine-learning development, quantum computing environments, supercomputing highly specialized environments, scientific highly specialized research and development environments, research and development for enterprise and government at any level of complexity [local to global], and many more).

  - Capable of hosting, and be hosted by, other environments (such as Microsoft SQL Server advanced data management system, Microsoft Visual Studio 2017, Microsoft Visual Studio 2019, and the Microsoft Azure set of advanced cloud products and services).

The CLI standard specification also includes an *intermediate assembly language*, and it is the Common Intermediate Language (CIL). Here is a necessary distinction:

- *Intermediate Language*: An IL is an abstract language used by a compiler as a step between program code and assembly code.

- *CIL*: The CIL is a formal instruction set to the CIL described in the CLI standard specification.

- *Microsoft Intermediate Language (MSIL)*: MSIL is Microsoft's implementation of the formal instruction set based on the ECMA-335 CIL described in the CLI standard specification.

When writing code using a programming language that adheres to the CLI standard specification, the result of the compiled code is a sequence of instructions of the CIL instruction set, as examples show in Listing 1-1 and Listing 1-2.

Open the sample solution RVJ.Core.sln at `<install_dir_on_your_local_computer>\Sources\APIs\DotNET\5.0\ProCustomLibs\Ch01\RVJ.Core\`.

In the first sample project (Buffers_Console_Client), we have in the Program.cs C# file a .NET custom data type named `Program` derived from `System.Object`, the .NET root data type for every kind of .NET concrete or abstract class or struct data type, directly or indirectly, as shown in Figure 1-2, Figure 1-3, and Figure 1-4, respectively.

In the C# programming language, because C# treats `System.Object` as the base class, we do not need to use the `System.Object` root data type explicitly when we do not have another class as the base data type.

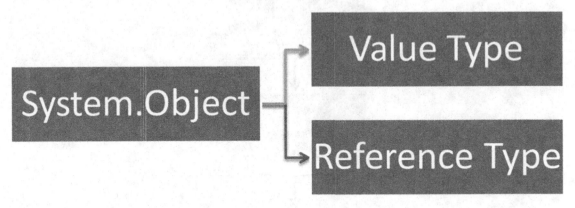

Figure 1-2. *Every .NET data type inherits, directly or indirectly, from the System. Object root data type. In .NET, we have a reference type and a value type*

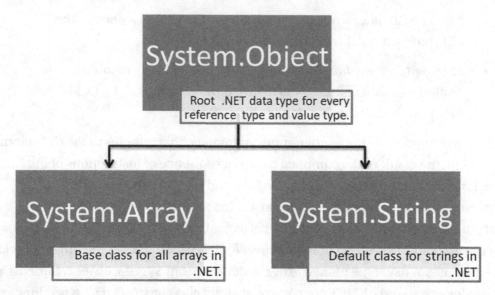

Figure 1-3. *Some .NET types (for example, System.Array) are abstract data types and are implemented partially by code generation of the compiler (for example, a C# compiler)*

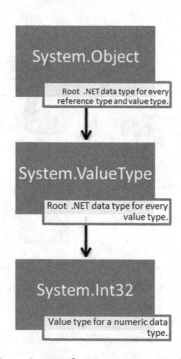

Figure 1-4. *System.ValueType is a reference type, and System.Int32 is a value type derived from System.ValueType, which inherits from the System.Object reference type*

In fact, the execution environment of the CLR (the VES) assumes this; therefore, most programming languages do not require that System.Object be informed explicitly in this scenario. However, it is good programming practice to explicitly use the base data type in such cases. Otherwise, this can become error prone when using more than one programming language in a project, potentially resulting in erroneous perceptions about the inheritance model supported by the .NET execution environment and the transfer of the desired feature to the programming language and the adoption of different programming languages (all because of basic resources of syntax).

Listing 1-1. Typical Source Code in the C# Programming Language for a Console Application with an Entry-Point Member Method Called Program.Main()

```
#region Namespaces
using System;
#endregion

namespace ConsoleClient {
    public static class Program : System.Object {
        public static void Main() {
            return;
        }
    };
};
```

Listing 1-2. Source Code in MSIL Generated in the Binary File, .EXE, or .DLL

```
.class public abstract auto ansi sealed beforefieldinit ConsoleClient.
Program
        extends [System.Runtime]System.Object {

.method public hidebysig static void  Main() cil managed {

  .entrypoint
  // Code size       1 (0x1)
  .maxstack  8
   ret

} // end of method Program::Main

} // end of class ConsoleClient.Program
```

These instructions are not for real hardware or processors. Instead, the CLI standard specification describes a virtual environment that includes some characteristics and functionalities of the elements available in a real computer.

.NET Platform

Microsoft .NET is the official commercial name for the group of technologies and tools designed and implemented based on what is in the ECMA-335 standard specification.

Common Language Runtime, as the name suggests, is an implementation based on the CLI standard specification, and an implementation of the CLR has a set of elements for a fundamental architectural model. Each element has a fundamental set of conceptual definitions and rules to be followed, and engineering mechanisms to be implemented, independently of the target operating system and hardware platforms.

When we are implementing a CLR environment and technologies of a .NET platform, we are creating software elements for a platform that is a nonspecific hardware-based computer (more specifically, a software-only computer, and more commonly known as a *virtual computer*). This description includes when planning and implementing custom data types, custom components, custom controls, custom libraries, and specialized tools and frameworks.

For this text, we are using a .NET 5 implementation of the CLR for the sample projects and respective source code.

You can check for the most up-to-date versions of .NET 5 at the official Microsoft website:

`https://dotnet.microsoft.com/download/dotnet/5.0.`

You can also use GitHub to access the source code of the runtime, libraries, and frameworks made using the CLR components and technologies and BCL fundamental library, as we have with Windows Forms (Microsoft Windows only), Windows Presentation Foundation (Microsoft Windows only), ASP.NET Core (Windows, Apple MacOS, Linux), and the .NET SDK Installer:

- `https://github.com/dotnet/runtime`

- `https://github.com/dotnet/aspnetcore`

- `https://github.com/dotnet/winforms`

- `https://github.com/dotnet/wpf`

- `https://github.com/dotnet/installer`

Independently or together, these abstract aspects focus on management of data types. So, reasonably, that form of environment and its components is known as a *managed environment*.

As mentioned previously, in this book we use a .NET 5 implementation of the CLR for the sample projects and respective source code. So, whenever you see CLR mentioned, this means the .NET 5 running on Microsoft Windows 10 2004 and Microsoft Visual Studio 2019 16.7.3 or more recent (Community, Professional, Enterprise). The following programming languages are used in this book:

- C#

- MSIL

For example, when we are developing some application and choose the `System.String` reference type, we are using one of the fundamental types available through the BCL.

However, the string reference type exists only because the CTS has the `string` fundamental built-in type defined on it, which is one of the platform-specific fundamental built-in types upon which string operations are built. In fact, the string content (value of) in any instance is made up of a sequence of values of the CTS `char` platform fundamental built-in type, which is `System.Char` fundamental data type in the BCL. These platform fundamental built-in types, BCL fundamental types, and any other types derived or based on them follow the rules described by the unified type system.

In the CLI specification, this unified type system is the CTS, which describes rules about conceptual, structural, and behavioral elements that must be followed by the CLI itself and specialized tools (such as compilers and runtime environments).

You'll learn more information about these types in Chapter 2 and in discussions about the CLR throughout this book. For now, though, Table 1-1 shows the types defined by the CTS and described by the metadata.

Table 1-1. *Fundamental Types Defined Through CTS*

BCL Types	CTS Types
C#	CIL/MSIL
System.Boolean	bool
System.Char	char
System.Object	object
System.String	string
System.Single	float32
System.Double	float64
System.SByte	int8
System.Int16	int16
System.Int32	int32
System.Int64	int64
System.IntPtr	native int
System.UIntPtr	native unsigned int
System.TypedReference	typedref
System.Byte	unsigned uint8
System.UInt16	unsigned uint16
System.UInt32	unsigned uint32
System.UInt64	unsigned uint64

Remember that this is not a one-to-one mapping between reserved words, data structures, specialized resources, or anything else in the programming languages. That is, what is formalized through the instructions in CIL, what is defined in the CLI specification, and what is implemented by the mechanisms on the platform is what prevails.

As a reminder, *unmanaged code* means executable and nonexecutable code that is not in CIL and is not under management and the rules of the CLR environment. Erroneously, the unmanaged code is often considered synonymous with native code; this is incorrect. For example, the CIL instruction set includes the following attributes:

- `cil` is a code implementation attribute that specifies that the method declaration and implementation consist only of CIL code (that is, managed code).

- `native` is a code implementation attribute that specifies that the method declaration and implementation consist only of native code (that is, native instructions of a specific hardware/processor platform). Currently, this functionality of the managed environment CLR implementation is used specifically as one of the base technologies of Platform Invoke (P/Invoke). P/Invoke is one of the mechanisms of the platform, and it is described in the CLI specification.

- `runtime` is a code implementation attribute that specifies that the implementation of the method be provided automatically by the runtime.

Two more of these attributes are available and can be combined with them:

- `managed` is a code implementation attribute that is used with methods for which implementation is written using only CIL code.

- `unmanaged` is a code implementation attribute that is used to describes that the implementation is not external. Currently, this code implementation attribute is used by P/Invoke technology, but it is not restricted to just that use.

The following implementation attributes are properly categorized as code implementation attributes:

- `cil`
- `native`
- `runtime`
- `managed`
- `unmanaged`

When unmanaged code needs to be used from the managed code, the unmanaged code implementation attribute must be applied on the method implementation. In the specific case of the P/Invoke mechanism, the use of the unmanaged code implementation attribute is required.

The pinvokeimpl method attribute is used to indicate that the runtime will switch from a managed state to an unmanaged state when executing the unmanaged code.

Listing 1-3 shows an example of a managed code implementation that uses an unmanaged code implementation of a well-known Windows application programming interface (API) HeapAlloc() function. The method has been applied the unmanaged and native code implementation attributes.

A switch from a managed state to an unmanaged state, and vice-versa, is performed automatically by the P/Invoke.

Listing 1-3. Excerpt in MSIL of Unmanaged Code (Using P/Invoke to Call the HeapAlloc() Function of Windows Memory Management, the Windows API)

```
.method assembly static pinvokeimpl( lasterr stdcall)
        void* modopt([mscorlib]System.Runtime.CompilerServices.
        CallConvStdcall)
        HeapAlloc(void* A_0,
                uint32 modopt([mscorlib]System.Runtime.CompilerServices.
                IsLong) A_1,
                uint32 modopt([mscorlib]System.Runtime.CompilerServices.
                IsLong) A_2) native unmanaged preservesig
{
  .custom instance void [mscorlib]System.Security.SuppressUnmanaged
  CodeSecurityAttribute::.ctor() = ( 01 00 00 00 )
  // Embedded native code
}
```

At this point, we have the following sequence of elements: the CLI standard specification that is composed by and describes the CTS group, the metadata group, the CLS and VES group, and the CLI itself.

About the Common Type System

When working with a sequence of bits, it is necessary to define the organization of these bits to do something useful. So, the data signified by the bit pattern should identify the data type (or a contextualized type based on the data).

The data type must have a purpose and contextually well-defined characteristics. For example, with regard to structural terms, the data type must have the required number of bits as defined and the fundamental operations that the type supports.

A type's conceptual, structural, and behavioral fundamental characteristics create a model as to what can be done and what cannot be done with any particular type: a type system model. Because the number of types is constantly increasing, a type system model is necessary to enforce rules to ensure that the environment works as designed and expected.

A type system model describes the necessary rules related to each type's conceptual, structural, and behavioral characteristics.

Fundamental Types and Hardware Platform

For this discussion, we use Intel IA-32/x64 and Intel 64 fundamental built-in data types (or fundamental built-in types), and we use some defined assembly instructions (implemented and supported) that derive the hardware architecture and the contextual interpretation of the bits on the data type.

The fundamental built-in data types are those defined as integral elements of the platform (in this case, the Intel IA-32/x64 and Intel 64 processor hardware architecture). Therefore, these types are integral elements of the hardware architecture and are not defined by an external library or execution environment.

These are the fundamental types:

- Byte (8 bits) (1 byte)

- Word (16 bits) (2 bytes)

- Doubleword (32-bits) (4 bytes)

- Quadword (64 bits) (8 bytes)

- Double quadword (128 bits) (16 bytes)

Although these fundamental built-in data types are supported by a common set of assembly instructions (such as MOV) that perform a common set of operations such move data from one place to another, some assembly instructions support additional interpretation of fundamental built-in data types.

The purpose of this additional interpretation is to allow numeric operations to be performed, and within this context these fundamental built-in data types are viewed and manipulated as numeric data types.

The Intel IA-32/x64 and Intel 64 processors recognize two integer types: signed and unsigned.

Assembly instructions such as ADD and SUB can perform operations on both signed integers and unsigned integers, but some assembly instructions can perform operations only with one type.

The Organization of Fundamental Data Types

Here are the bits as a single pattern, without additional rules or interpretation, except for the fundamental requirements of the hardware platform:

- Byte (8 bits)
  - Bits 7...0
- Word (16 bits)
  - Bits 15...0
  - Bits 15...8 (high byte)
  - Bits 7...0 (low byte)
- Doubleword (32 bits)
  - Bits 31...0
  - Bits 31...16 (high word)
  - Bits 15...0 (low word)
- Quadword (64 bits)
  - Bits 63...0
  - Bits 63...32 (high doubleword)
  - Bits 31...0 (low doubleword)

- Double quadword (128 bits)

  - Bits 127...0

  - Bits 127...64 (high quadword)

  - Bits 63...0 (low quadword)

Table 1-2 describes the bits in more detail, including information about fundamental hardware requirements and integer types (signed and unsigned).

Table 1-2. *Fundamental Data Types*

Numeric Data Type	Description
Byte unsigned integer	All bits used to represent the value. Values range from 0 to 255. (2^8-1)
Word unsigned integer	All bits used to represent the value. Values range from 0 to 65,535. $(2^{16}-1)$
Doubleword unsigned integer	All bits used to represent the value. Values range from 0 to 4,294,967,295. $(2^{32}-1)$
Quadword unsigned integer	All bits used to represent the value. Values range from 0 to 18,446,744,073,709,551,615. $(2^{64}-1)$
Byte signed integer	The first 7 bits (6...0) used to represent the value, the most significant bit (MSB) used as the signed bit. When the MSB has value 0, the number is positive. When the MSB has value 1, the number is negative. Values range from -128 to +127.

(continued)

15

Table 1-2. (*continued*)

Numeric Data Type	Description
Word signed integer	The first 15 bits (14…0) used to represent the value, he MSB used as the signed bit . When the MSB has value 0, the number is positive. When the MSB has value 1, the number is negative. Values range from -32,768 to +32,767.
Doubleword signed integer	The first 31 bits (30…0) used to represent the value, the MSB used as the signed bit. When the MSB has value 0, the number is positive. When the MSB has value 1, the number is negative. Values range from -2^{31} to $+2^{31}-1$.
Quadword signed integer	The first 63 bits (62…0) used to represent the value, the MSB used as the signed bit When the MSB has value 0, the number is positive. When the MSB has value 1, the number is negative. Values range from -2^{63} to $+2^{63}-1$.

CTS for Fundamental Types

The CTS supports types that describe values and types that specify contracts (behaviors that the type supports), and the support for these types must be present in an implementation of a CLR. These two types are supported because one of the principles of the CTS is to support object-oriented programming (OOP), procedural, and functional programming languages.

A value is a bit pattern used to represent types such as numbers (for example, integer numbers and float-pointing numbers).

Listing 1-4 shows examples in C# for two variables for instances of the System. UInt32 BCL value type (and not a simple value).

Listing 1-4. C# Examples Declaring Variables Using uint and System.UInt32, the Same Kind of Object (An Instance of the Value Type of System.UInt32 Data Type of BCL)

```
const uint LimitOne = 72; // C# code.
const System.UInt32 LimitTwo = 144; // C# code.

Console.WriteLine( "{0}", LimitTwo.ToString() );
```

A value type is not an object type, but it is defined using a class definition (declaration and implementation).

Remember that this way of work is defined by CTS and supported by VES in the CLR. From the perspective of the type system and execution environment, it is necessary that an object be declared, defined, and implemented to work within the CLR.

Table 1-3 describes the fundamental built-in types defined by CTS. As the table shows, the root object type is accessible through the object keyword of the CIL. So that programming languages such as C#, C++/CLI projection, F#, VB.NET, and others can access this root object type of the platform, there is a library of fundamental types that is part of the CLI specification. This foundational library is the BCL.

Table 1-3. CTS System.Object (Root Managed Object Type)

BCL Types		CTS Types
C++/CLI projection	**C# programming language**	CIL
System::Object^ (same root managed object type)	C# object is the keyword used for CTS/BCL System.Object (same root managed object type)	object (same root managed object type)

This root object type is the System.Object reference type. When declaring a variable of the object type (CTS model definition) or System.Object (BCL) reference type using any high-level programming language such as C#, C++/CLI projection, F#, VB.NET, and so on, the compiler generates an intermediate code using the object keyword of the CIL. Table 1-4 summarizes and helps you understand and memorize this sequence in a straightforward way.

Table 1-4. *Contextual Resources and Their Fundamental Purposes*

Your .NET specialized applications	Applications, services, components, libraries, and frameworks.
.NET	Software development kit (SDK, a specialized tools for software development, analysis, deployment, and some types of management) Specialized components, libraries, and frameworks
CLR	Implementation of a specialized managed environment based of CLI specification Uses the resources of the underlying hardware and operating system platform (for example, Microsoft Windows operating system) Adaptable and capable of using the specialized resources of the underlying hardware and operating system (for example, Microsoft Windows 10, Microsoft Windows Server 2016, Linux distributions, Apple iOS, and Apple MacOS.

Virtual Execution System

The VES provides an environment for running managed code, security boundaries, and memory management.

Two fundamental built-in types (string and array) are used as a starting point in this discussion to explain various aspects of CTS and VES.

These platform built-in fundamental types are present in any kind of software, so they stand as orthogonal elements.

However, the .NET platform also has a special foundational library, also part of the CLI specification, that supplies specialized types necessary to design and implement any kind of software: the BCL.

As we explore the the organization of the BCL, we'll use the `System.Object`, `System.String`, and `System.Array` reference types as starting points and deconstruct many aspects of their implementation. This discussion will then enable us to explore the interface types implemented by these types in various specialized frameworks (such as Windows Forms, Windows Presentation Foundation [WPF], Universal Windows Platform [UWP] applications, and ASP.NET).

The VES provides direct support for a set of platform-specific built-in fundamental types, defines a hypothetical machine with an associated machine model and state, and provides a set of control flow constructs and an exception-handling model.

To a considerable extent, the purpose of the VES is to provide the support required to execute the MSIL instruction set.

The VES is the system that implements and enforces the CTS model. For example, the VES is responsible for loading and running programs written to CLI.

The VES provides the services needed to execute managed code and data using the metadata to connect separately generated modules together at runtime. The VES is also known as the execution engine.

.NET Module

When we use C++ to write code, the result of the compiled and linked code is a binary file in a specific format. In this case, we are working with PE/COFF (Portable Executable / Common Object File Format), which is used by the Microsoft Windows operating system. When we use C# to write code, or when we use any other programming language or group of extensions that adhere to the CLI specification, the resulting binary file is in the same PE/COFF format. However, that resulting binary file has some data structures changed/included to support the requirements described by CLI specification and aspects of the Microsoft Windows operating system. This is called the *CLI PE/COFF module*.

Currently, on Microsoft Windows, the CLI PE/COFF module can have .EXE, .DLL, .netmodule, .WinMD, and .UWP extensions created and recognized by the operation system or development tools. In addition, it can have any other extension that can be registered and recognized by the operating system or specialized tools (for software development or not).

In fact, the use of an extension is not required, but it is a good practice and the accepted standard.

If we are using .NET 5 or .NET Core (*not* the old Windows-only .NET Framework) in a different operating system and on a different hardware platform, the extensions and file formats used are specific to such software and hardware environments. However, the fundamental structural resources defined in CLI as a starting point are the same.

One VES responsibility is to load the CLI PE/COFF modules. Doing so includes verifying some structural rules about the file format and guaranteeing that all information is as expected. The VES uses the metadata information in the CLI PE/COFF modules to verify that the structural aspects are recognized by the rules that it knows as valid, required, or optional. If the structural elements exist and are valid, the next step is to apply the rules based on the nature of the elements and the context of use.

For example, if the element is a managed type, the execution system needs to verify whether it is a value type or a reference type.

If the element is an assembly reference type, one responsibility of this type is to describe various characteristics of the managed module (structural and behavioral), such as the relationships it has with other managed modules and what managed types are in it (and in any other managed module).

.NET Assemblies

People often wonder what a .NET assembly is exactly. Put simply, and as defined and described by the CLI, an assembly is a logical unit for management and deployment of resources designed to work together. In an implementation of CLR, assemblies can be static or dynamic.

Static Assemblies

Static assemblies are those stored in a storage device, such as a typical hard disk. In Microsoft Windows, the file format of each module is the CLI PE/COFF. These assemblies have typical .NET 5 types and other specialized resources (audio/video files, localization support files, images, and custom files created specifically for the application), depending on the purpose of each application. .NET 5 and .NET Core include the following assemblies and modules, for example:

- Assembly `mscorlib`
    - Module `mscorlib.dll`
    - Module `System.Runtime.dll`
    - Module `netstandard.dll`
- Assembly `System.Activities` (part of Microsoft Windows Workflow Foundation)
    - Module `System.Activities.dll`

- Assembly System.Diagnostics.Debug

  - Module System.Diagnostics.Debug.dll

  - Module System.dll

  - Module netstandard.dll

Dynamic Assemblies

Dynamic assemblies are created dynamically at runtime and are created via specialized API calls of .NET 5/Core. These dynamic assemblies are created and executed directly in memory. However, the dynamic assembly can be saved in a storage device, but only after being executed.

In a typical project, though, we have many files—binary files with executable code or binary files with other types of data (for example, images)—that are part of the software. Therefore, the description, verification, and reinforcement of the relations and dependencies among them are made in part by the metadata.

Metadata is partly responsible for making resources available to perform these tasks.

Working with Assemblies and Modules

For a static assembly or a dynamic assembly, the principles prevails, a way of keep the cohesiveness of the types and resources designed to work together. Deployment, Execution and Management. The information stored in the modules and created through assemblies is what helps the runtime environment understand and apply the rules to the relations among the elements.

Let's use a typical static assembly.

There are four elements:

- CIL, that implements all the types and required logic to the module

- Metadata

- The resources (audio/video files, localization support files, images and custom files created specifically for the application)

- The assembly manifest

From the perspective of the runtime environment and basic structural rules described in the CLI, of these four elements, only the assembly manifest is a required item. However, considering even the simplest application or component, if we do not have the other elements, the application or component does not have a practical use (except for learning about the assemblies and modules, which I consider a quite practical use).

Organization of Elements in a Module (Physical File)

We start with a basic example here and continue with more details in Chapter 2.

Follow these steps:

1. Using the code editor of your preference, create a simple file and save it with the name **RVJ.ProDotNETCustomLibs.il** in the directory of your choice that can be used to build source code.

2. Open (as administrator) one of the developer command prompts installed and configured by Microsoft Visual Studio 2019.

3. Copy the following sequence of MSIL code into the file RVJ. ProDotNETCustomLibs.il and save the file:

```
.assembly extern System.Runtime {
  .ver 5:0:0:0
}

.assembly RVJ.ProDotNETCustomLibs.Buffers {

.ver 1:0:0:0

}
```

4. In the developer command prompt, write the following command:

```
ilasm /DLL /Output=RVJ.ProDotNETCustomLibs.dll
RVJ.ProDotNETCustomLibs.il
```

If the code compiles without error, the output will be a binary file with the name RVJ.ProDotNETCustomLibs.dll.

By following these steps, we have created a *single-file static assembly,* with only the assembly manifest.

Using the ILDASM Tool

With the code compiled and the binary generated, we now can use the Intermediate Language Disassembler (ILDASM) tool. (ISLASM, in contrast, stands for Intermediate Language Assembler.) On the same command prompt that we used to compile the code, write the following command:

```
ildasm RVJ.ProDotNETCustomLibs.dll
```

With the module `RVJ.ProDotNETCustomLibs.dll` loaded by the ILDasm.exe tool, we see the screen shown in Figure 1-5.

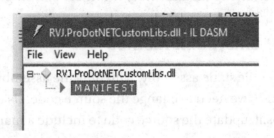

Figure 1-5. *ILDASM showing a single-file static assembly*

Now double-click in the manifest. A new window will open with information about the assembly manifest, as shown in Figure 1-6.

```
// Metadata version: v4.0.30319
.assembly extern System.Runtime
{
  .ver 5:0:0:0
}
.assembly RVJ.ProDotNETCustomLibs.Buffers
{
  .ver 1:0:0:0
}
.module RVJ.ProDotNETCustomLibs.dll
// MVID: {4F3F4E2D-1B19-438C-AF57-B83ECC43CCAF}
.imagebase 0x00400000
.file alignment 0x00000200
.stackreserve 0x00100000
.subsystem 0x0003       // WINDOWS_CUI
.corflags 0x00000001    //   ILONLY
// Image base: 0x0B820000
```

Figure 1-6. ILDASM showing the assembly manifest of a single-file static assembly

Implementing the entrypoint Method

We have created a single-file static assembly, with only the assembly manifest. If we want to create an .EXE, we need to change the source code. Using the same RVJ. ProDotNETCustomLibs.il, update the source code to include a managed method that is the entry point:

```
.assembly extern System.Runtime {
  .ver 5:0:0:0
}
.assembly RVJ.ProDotNETCustomLibs.Buffers {

.ver 1:0:0:0

}

.method static public void MyEntryPointMethod() cil managed {

.entrypoint

    ret
}
```

As you can see, the name of the `.entrypoint` method does not need to be `main`. To build this code, use the following command:

```
ilasm /Output=RVJ.ProDotNETCustomLibs.exe RVJ.ProDotNETCustomLibs.il
```

After the code compiles without error and with the binary generated, we can use the ILDasm.exe tool to load the module `RVJ.ProDotNETCustomLibs.exe`, and then we have more than just the assembly manifest, as shown in Figure 1-7.

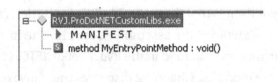

Figure 1-7. *ILDASM showing a single-file static assembly*

As shown in Figure 1-8, we have created a single-file static assembly, with the assembly manifest and one method (in this case, the entry-point method). When `RVJ.DotNETProCustomLibs.exe` runs, it runs like any other .NET managed executable.

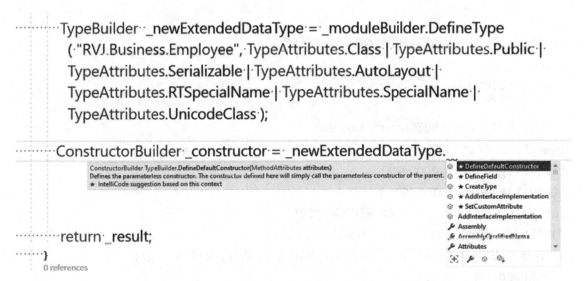

Figure 1-8. *ILDASM showing a single-file static assembly, with the assembly manifest and one managed method*

Listing 1-5 shows an example of managed instructions from one of the sample projects that comes with the companion content of this book. The .module directive indicates the name of the binary module (in this case, RVJ.ProDotNETCustomLibs. exe). The .assembly directive describes which assemblies make this a logical unit of management and deployment of resources designed to work together. The .assembly RVJ. ProDotNETCustomLibs.Buffers (without the extern keyword) describes that this assembly is in the current module. The use of .assembly extern directive describes to the assembly the types that your .assembly or .module are referencing. For example, .assembly extern System.Runtime indicates that the assembly RVJ.ProDotNETCustomLibs. Buffers is using one or more types of the assembly mscorlib. The highlighted CIL instructions are the same that you can read in the RVJ.ProDotNETCustomLibs.dll or RVJ. ProDotNETCustomLibs.exe modules. Chapter 2 discusses these and other instructions in more detail (with even fuller detail following in subsequent chapters).

Listing 1-5. Fundamental Keywords Used by Static Assemblies or Dynamic Assemblies

```
.assembly extern System.Runtime {
  .ver 5:0:0:0
}

.assembly RVJ.ProDotNETCustomLibs.Buffers
{
  .ver 1:0:0:0
}
.module RVJ.ProDotNETCustomLibs.exe
.imagebase 0x00400000
.file alignment 0x00000200
.stackreserve 0x00100000
.subsystem 0x0003        // WINDOWS_CUI
.corflags 0x00000001     // ILONLY
.method public static void  MyEntryPointMethod() cil managed {
  .entrypoint
  // Code size        1 (0x1)
  .maxstack  8
  IL_0000:  ret
} // end of method 'Global Functions'::MyEntryPointMethod
```

As you can see, the VES handles a lot of work. Even still, though, there are more interesting functionalities within this mechanism.

Chapter 2 discusses these resources and goes into more detail about the CTS and VES. Specifically, you'll read more about fundamental built-in types and about how the execution environment deals with these types and structural elements of the platform. Initially, we use code written directly in CIL to provide more information about the use of the types and so that you better understand how to work with modules and assemblies. We then use some code in C++ to highlight some internal aspects of the execution environment and some special types. From that point, we embark on our journey through foundational BCL using the MSIL and C# programming languages.

CHAPTER 2

Custom .NET Data Type

This chapter covers implementation methods that a .NET custom data type inherits from the System.Object root .NET data type.

Management of Data Types

A Common Language Runtime (CLR) implementation involves a set of elements for a fundamental architectural model. Each element has an essential conceptual definitions and rules to follow and engineering mechanisms to implement (regardless of the target operating system and hardware platforms).

In fact, when we are planning and implementing data types, components, and libraries for an implementation of a CLR environment and technologies of a .NET platform, we are creating software elements for a nonspecific hardware-based computer, a software-only computer more specifically, or a virtual computer as it is more commonly called (as you learned in Chapter 1).

The CLR, as its name suggests, is an implementation based on the official ECMA-335 Common Language Infrastructure (CLI) specification. In this book, we use a .NET 5 implementation of the CLR for the sample projects and respective source code.

Working with System.Object, the Root of .NET Reference Types

System.Object is the .NET full name of the managed root type from which all managed and unmanaged .NET data types derive (directly, indirectly, implicitly, or explicitly).

As shown in Figure 2-1, in a .NET platform we have two fundamental conceptual data types: reference types and value types.

R. Villela, *Pro .NET 5 Custom Libraries*, https://doi.org/10.1007/978-1-4842-6391-4_2

The reference type is the root for every kind of .NET data type. For example, the value and interface types are a specialization of the reference type. All kinds of .NET data types inherit, implicitly or explicitly, fundamental characteristics of a reference type.

The fundamental difference for the implementation of each kind of .NET data type is the contextual comprehension of the execution environment of the CLR about the .NET data type in use and the applied standards of the ECMA-335 specification.

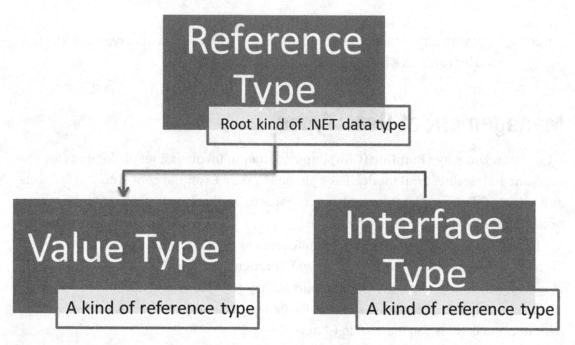

Figure 2-1. *Reference type is the root for every kind of .NET data type*

Another typical characteristic of a .NET data type is the support for the implementation of multiple .NET interfaces for the same data type. That is, the same .NET data type can implement multiple contracts.

As of this writing, we cannot have a .NET data type with support for multiple inheritance as defined in object-oriented programming (OOP). That is, the same .NET data type inherits from more than one .NET class type at the same level in the hierarchy.

A reference type is always a class/object or interface type. An interface type is a kind of type derived from a conceptual reference type. A value type is always a structure data type. Both inherit from the System.Object root .NET reference type, as shown in Figure 2-2.

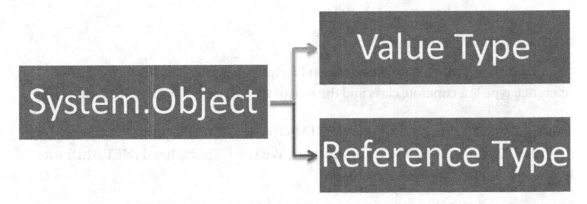

Figure 2-2. *System.Object is the root .NET type for all value and reference types*

For example, System.Array (and all arrays) derives from the System.Array abstract reference type that is part of the Common Type System (CTS), directly supported by the Virtual Execution System (VES), described and supported in the metadata, and part of the Common Language Specification (CLS), as discussed in Chapter 1.

In the CLR execution environment implementation, the reference type is always allocated space in heap memory. Because of this, it is called a *heap-based data type* and is recommended for more complex data types with long-lived instances, which are not necessarily deallocated when out of scope, including a nested block scope, when supported by a programming language in use.

In a .NET Base Class Library (BCL) implementation, every .NET reference type has a root data type, which for .NET is the System.Object reference type, also part of every .NET BCL implementation for any target environment.

At the time of this writing, the .NET System.Object reference type is a piece of the following .NET assemblies/modules:

- .NET 5 (System.Runtime.dll)

- .NET Core (System.Runtime.dll)

- .NET Framework (mscorlib.dll)

- .NET Standard (netstandard.dll)

- UWP (System.Runtime.dll)

- Xamarin.Android (mscorlib.dll)

- Xamarin.iOS (`mscorlib.dll`)

- Xamarin.Mac (`mscorlib.dll`)

As shown in Listing 2-1, Listing 2-2, and Figure 2-3, the `System.Object` .NET reference type is a concrete class and the root of all .NET reference and .NET value types:

Listing 2-1. For the .NET Framework (Microsoft Windows Only), Xamarin. Android, Xamarin.iOS, and Xamarin.Mac, We Have Specialized .NET Attributes Explicitly Applied for Implementation

```
[System.Runtime.InteropServices.ClassInterface(System.Runtime.
InteropServices.ClassInterfaceType.AutoDual)]
[System.Runtime.InteropServices.ComVisible(true)]
[System.Serializable]
public class System.Object{}
```

Listing 2-2. For .NET 5, .NET Core, .NET Standard, and UWP, We Have No .NET Attributes Explicitly Applied for Implementation

```
public class System.Object{}
```

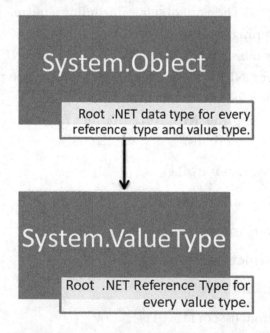

Figure 2-3. *Concrete classes: The System.Object is the root of all .NET reference types and, the System.ValueType is the root of all .NET value types*

Listing 2-3, Listing 2-4, and Figure 2-4 show the following examples implemented in the .NET BCL:

- `System.Array`

- `System.Attribute`

- `System.Buffer`

- `System.Console`

- `System.Delegate`

- `System.Environment`

- `System.Exception`

- `System.FormattableString`

- `System.MulticastDelegate`

- `System.Nullable`

- `System.String`

Also, we have more specialized derivations of a `System.Object` as part of the .NET BCL and .NET Framework Class Library (FCL), including the following:

- `System.Memory<T>`

- `System.OperatingSystem`

- `System.Predicate<in T>`

- `System.Uri`

- `System.ValueType` (the root abstract class for all value types)

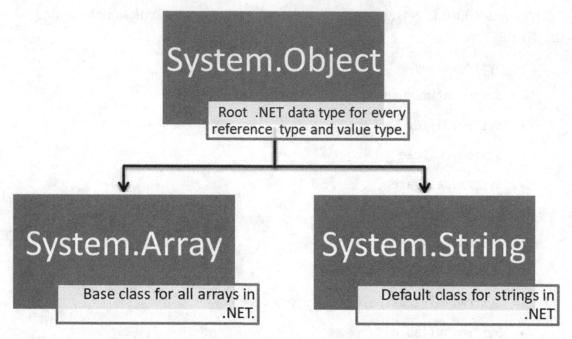

Figure 2-4. *.NET BCL has implemented as a derivation of System.Object common types such as System.Array and System.String*

Listing 2-3. For the .NET Framework (Microsoft Windows only), Xamarin. Android, Xamarin.iOS, and Xamarin.Mac, we have Specialized .NET Attributes Explicitly Applied for Implementation

```
[System.Runtime.InteropServices.ComVisible(true)]
[System.Serializable]
public abstract class System.Array : System.ICloneable, System.Collections.
IList, System.Collections.IStructuralComparable, System.Collections.
IStructuralEquatable

[System.Runtime.InteropServices.ComVisible(true)]
[System.Serializable]
public sealed class System.String : System.ICloneable, System.IComparable,
System.IComparable <System.String>, System.IConvertible, System.
IEquatable<System.String>, System.Collections.Generic.IEnumerable<System.Char>
```

Listing 2-4. For .NET 5, .NET Core, .NET Standard, and UWP, We Have No .NET Attributes Explicitly Applied for Implementation

```
public abstract class System.Array : System.ICloneable, System.Collections.
IList, System.Collections.IStructuralComparable, System.Collections.
IStructuralEquatable
```

```
public sealed class System.String : System.ICloneable, System.IComparable,
System.IComparable <System.String>, System.IConvertible, System.
IEquatable<System.String>, System.Collections.Generic.IEnumerable<System.Char>
```

System.ValueType, the Root of .NET Value Types

In a CLR execution environment implementation, a value type is always allocated in stack memory. Because of this characteristic, it is also called a stack-based data type, and it is recommended (when supported by the programming language in use) for noncomplex custom data types with short-lived instances that are deallocated when out of scope, including when used in a nested block scope.

In the .NET BCL implementation, every .NET value type has the root data type System.ValueType reference type, which is also part of every .NET BCL implementation for any target environment.

System.ValueType is a .NET reference type declared as an abstract class and derives directly from the System.Object .NET reference type, as shown in Listing 2-5, Listing 2-6, and Figure 2-5.

Listing 2-5. For .NET Framework (Microsoft Windows Only), Xamarin.Android, Xamarin.iOS, and Xamarin.Mac, We Have Specialized .NET Attributes Explicitly Applied for Implementation

```
[System.Runtime.InteropServices.ComVisible(true)]
[System.Serializable]
public abstract class System.ValueType: System.Object {}
```

Listing 2-6. For .NET 5, .NET Core, .NET Standard, and UWP, We Have No .NET Attributes Explicitly Applied for Implementation

```
public abstract class System.ValueType: System.Object {}
```

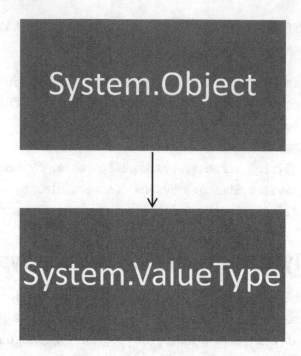

Figure 2-5. *The System.ValueType .NET reference type is declared as an abstract class and derives directly from the System.Object .NET reference type*

As shown in Listing 2-7, Listing 2-8, and Figure 2-6, in .NET BCL we have fundamental types implemented as a derivation of `System.ValueType`, including the following few example:

- `System.Byte`

- `System.SByte`

- `System.UInt32`

- `System.Int32`

- `System.UInt16`

- `System.Int16`

- `System.UInt64`

- `System.Int64`

- `System.Single`

- `System.Double`

- `System.Decimal`

Also, we have more specialized derivations of a `System.ValueType` as part of the .NET BCL and .NET FCL, including the following:

- `System.Boolean`

- `System.Char`

- `System.Enum`

- `System.DateTime`

- `System.Text.Rune` (introduced in .NET Core 3.0)

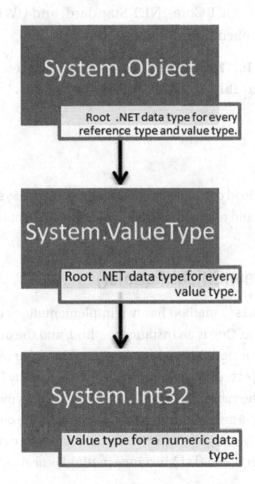

Figure 2-6. *Inheritance model for the .NET System.Int32 value type and base classes*

Listing 2-7. For .NET Framework (Microsoft Windows), Xamarin.Android, Xamarin.iOS, and Xamarin.Mac, We Have Specialized .NET Attributes Explicitly Applied for Implementation

```
[System.Runtime.InteropServices.ComVisible(true)]
[System.Serializable]
public struct System.Int32: System.IComparable, System.IComparable<System.
Int32>, System.IConvertible, System.IEquatable<System.Int32>, System.
IFormattable
```

Listing 2-8. For .NET 5, .NET Core, .NET Standard, and UWP, We Have No .NET Attributes Explicitly Applied for Implementation

```
public struct System.Int32 : System.IComparable, System.IComparable<System.
Int32>, System.IConvertible, System.IEquatable<System.Int32>, System.
IFormattable
```

Methods

We should override/overload certain inherited methods of the System.Object for our .NET custom data types, and not work with default inherited implementations of the base types.

Working with System.Object.Equals()

The System.Object.Equals() method has two implementations that we can access for our .NET custom data type. One is an instance method, and the other is a static method.

We access the instance method because, firstly, we have our .NET custom data type derived from System.Object, directly or indirectly, and secondly because the instance method is defined with the public keyword, which is an access modifier.

As shown by Listing 2-9 and Listing 2-10, we should use the override access modifier keyword on the instance method in our .NET custom-derived data type because the System.Object.Equals() instance method is also defined with the virtual access modifier keyword.

If the instance method were defined with only the `public` access modifier keyword but not with the `virtual` access modifier keyword, our .NET custom-derived data type could access the instance method, but it could not override it using the implementation model provided by CLR for virtual methods.

Listing 2-9. The Instance Method Is Also Defined with the Virtual Access Modifier Keyword

```
public virtual System.Boolean Equals( System.Object );
```

We should use the `override` access modifier keyword because our specialization of `System.Object` (or another .NET data type) is creating a contextual logic and requires specialized verifications too, as shown in Listing 2-10.

Listing 2-10. Using the override Access Modifier Keyword for Our Specialization

```
namespace RVJ.Core.Business {

    public class Person : System.Object {

        #region Private fields
        private System.Guid _internal_ID;
        private UInt32 _age;
        private String _firstName;
        private String _lastName;
        #endregion

        #region Constructor(s)

        public Person() : base() {

            this._internal_ID = System.Guid.NewGuid();
            this._age = new UInt32();
            this._firstName = String.Empty;
            this._lastName = String.Empty;

            return;
        }
        #endregion

        #region Override System.Object.Equals()
```

```csharp
    public override Boolean Equals( System.Object instance ) {

        // An instance of Person or derivation of it
        Person _another = ( instance as Person );
        Boolean _equals = ( ( _another != null ) &&
        ( this._internal_ID == _another._internal_ID )
        && System.Object.ReferenceEquals( this, _another ) );

        return _equals;
    }

#endregion
                    #region New implementation for System.Object.
                    ReferenceEquals()
                    public new static System.Boolean ReferenceEquals
                    ( System.Object first, System.Object second ) {

                            // An instance of Person or derivation
                                Person _first = ( first as Person );
                                Person _second = ( second as Person );
                                Boolean _equals = ( ( ( _first !=
                                null ) && ( _second != null ) ) &&
                                ( _first._internal_ID.Equals
                                ( _second._internal_ID ) && System.
                                Object.ReferenceEquals
                                ( _first,  _second ) ) );

                    return _equals;
                    }
                #endregion

    #region Overrides System.Object.GetHashCode()
    public override Int32 GetHashCode() {
        return System.HashCode.Combine<Int32>( base.GetHashCode() );
        //return base.GetHashCode();
    }
    #endregion
    };

};
```

Our `RVJ.Core.Business.Person.Equals()` instance method is a mix of fundamental and required rules of the CLR execution environment and specialized contextual rules that are specific to our .NET custom data type.

To be considered equals, two instances of a .NET reference type should be of the same lineage at some point in the planned hierarchy. For example, an instance of `RVJ.Core.Business.Person` or of a derivation of it can be compared only with another instance of `RVJ.Core.Business.Person` or a derivation of it (directly or indirectly).

The `System.Object.ReferenceEquals()` public static method is used because it verifies whether we are pointing to the same instance. That is, it verifies whether we are trying to compare `_instanceOfPerson.Equals(this)` or `RVJ.Core.Business.Person.Equals(this, this)` when using the static method, because both expressions should always return true.

This sounds unnecessary, but it should be considered part of the rules because of security. If part of the metadata of an instance were to be corrupted by an attack of some kind, the expressions `_instanceOfPerson.Equals(this)` and `RVJ.Core.Business.Person.Equals(this, this)` will not work when using the static method (as explained here and as defined by ECMA-335 specification rules for CLR implementations).

With these fundamental verifications, we are also introducing rules specific to our .NET custom data type. Up to this point, only the concept of *internal ID* has been introduced, but our specialization can introduce others, as required.

As shown in Listing 2-11 and Listing 2-12, `System.Object.Equals()` has another implementation that we can access because it is `public` and `static`.

Listing 2-11. System.Object.Equals() Also Has an Implementation Defined as public and static

```
public static System.Boolean Equals( System.Object, System.Object );
```

Because it is a `static` member, we don't need an instance to access the member. Because we are working with the relationship and inheritance, however, this is considered by .NET rules an inherited member, and we can hide this specific `System.Object.Equals()` implementation by using the `new` access modifier keyword.

As shown in Listing 2-12, we should create for our .NET custom data types a specialized implementation using the `new` access modifier keyword that hides the inherited behavior.

Listing 2-12. Specialized Implementation Using the new Access Modifier
Keyword for Our Custom .NET Data Type

```
#region Namespaces/Assemblies
using System;
#endregion

namespace RVJ.Core.Business {

    public class Person : System.Object {

        #region Private fields
        private System.Guid _internal_ID;
        private UInt32 _age;
        private String _firstName;
        private String _lastName;
        #endregion

        #region Constructor(s)
        public Person() : base() {

            this._internal_ID = System.Guid.NewGuid();
            this._age = new UInt32();
            this._firstName = String.Empty;
            this._lastName = String.Empty;

            return;
        }
        #endregion

        #region Override System.Object.Equals()

        public override Boolean Equals( System.Object instance ) {

            // An instance of Person or derivation
            Person _another = ( instance as Person );
            Boolean _equals = ( ( _another != null ) && ( this._internal_ID
            == _another._internal_ID ) && System.Object.ReferenceEquals(
            this, _another ) );
```

```
        return _equals;
    }

public new static Boolean Equals( System.Object first, System.
Object second ) {

    // An instance of Person or derivation
    Person _first = ( first as Person );
    Person _second = ( second as Person );

    /* Boolean _equals = ( ( _first != null ) && ( _second != null )
    && ( ( _first._internal_ID == _second._internal_ID ) ) &&
    System.Object.ReferenceEquals( _first, _second ) ); */
                                    // This expression implements
                                    the expression above.
    return ( (_first != null ) ? _first.Equals( _second ) : _
    second.Equals( _first ) ) ;
}

#endregion

#region Overrides System.Object.GetHashCode()
public override Int32 GetHashCode() {
    return System.HashCode.Combine<Int32>( base.GetHashCode() );
    //return base.GetHashCode();
}
#endregion

    };

};
```

Listing 2-13 shows examples of expressions that check the RVJ.Core.Business. Person.Equals() instance and static operation implementations.

Listing 2-13. Expressions for RVJ.Core.Business.Person.Equals() Instance and Static Operation Implementations

```
Person _personA = new Person();
Person _personB = new Person();

#region RVJ.Core.Business.Person.Equals() operation

// Must be false
Boolean _areEquals = _personA.Equals( _personB);

// Must be false
_areEquals = _personB.Equals( _personA);

// Must be false
_areEquals = _personA.Equals(null);

// Must be false
_areEquals = _personB.Equals(null);

// Must be false
_areEquals = _personA.Equals(new Object());

// Must be false
_areEquals = _personB.Equals(new Object() ;

// Must be false
_areEquals = _personA.Equals( _ = new Object());

// Must be false
_areEquals = _personB.Equals( _ = new Object());

// Must be false
_areEquals = _personA.Equals( _ = new Person());

// Must be false
_areEquals = _personB.Equals( _ = new Person());

// Must be false
_areEquals = _personA.Equals( _ = new Int32());
```

```
// Must be false
_areEquals = _personB.Equals( _ = new Int32());

// Must be false
_areEquals = _personA.Equals( _ = _personB);

// Must be false
_areEquals = _personB.Equals( _ = _personA);

// Must be false
_areEquals = ( _ = _personA ).Equals( _personB);

// Must be false
_areEquals = ( _ = _personB ).Equals( _personA);

// Must be true
_areEquals = _personA.Equals( _personA);

// Must be true
_areEquals = _personB.Equals( _personB);

// Must be true
_areEquals = _personA.Equals( _ = _personA );

// Must be true
_areEquals = _personB.Equals( _ = _personB );

// Must be true
_areEquals = ( _ = _personA ).Equals( _personA);

// Must be true
_areEquals = ( _ = _personB ).Equals( _personB);

#endregion
```

Operators == and != for Equality and Inequality Behaviors

An equality operation is implemented through the == operator, and an inequality
operation is implemented through the != operator, as shown in Listing 2-14.

When implementing a .NET custom data type that overrides System.Object. Equals(), as we have with RVJ.Core.Business.Person, we should also implement the == and != operators.

Listing 2-14. Implementing == and != Operators

```
#region Operators Equality ==  and Inequality !=

        public static Boolean operator ==( Person first, Person second ) {
            return Person.ReferenceEquals( first, second );
        }
        public static Boolean operator !=( Person first, Person second ) {
            return !Person.ReferenceEquals( first, second );
        }

#endregion
```

Because we have a good implementation for the RVJ.Core.Business.Person. Equals() instance and static methods, our implementations for the == and != operators are very objective. Because we are working with static methods for == and != operators as required by .NET, we are using our implementation of the RVJ.Core.Business. Person.ReferenceEquals() static method for the work.

Working with System.Object.GetHashCode()

System.Object.GetHashCode() is an inheritable instance method for a default hash function, and it is defined with public and virtual access modifier keywords.

When we have our .NET custom data type, it is important to have our specialized implementation for System.Object.GetHashCode() with the default method implementation.

According to the official Microsoft guidelines for this method, when we override System.Object.Equals(System.Object) we must also override System.Object. GetHashCode(). Doing so helps guarantee that hash tables will work correctly, for example.

Listing 2-15. Default Signature for Implementation for Hash Code of the System. Object Root Class

```
public virtual System.Int32 GetHashCode();
```

As shown in Listings 2.15 and 2.16, a rule that applies to the System.Object. GetHashCode() method is that when we have a specialized implementation for System.Object.Equals() methods, as we have with the RVJ.Core.Business.Person .NET custom data type, we must have an implementation for the System.Object. GetHashCode() default method implementation.

Listing 2-16 shows our custom implementation for the RVJ.Core.Business.Person. GetHashCode() instance method.

Listing 2-16. Custom Implementation for Hash Code Using the System. HashCode Reference Type

```
#region Namespaces/Assemblies
using System;
#endregion

namespace RVJ.Core.Business {
    public class Person : System.Object {
         #region Private fields
        private Guid _internal_ID;
        private UInt32 _age;
        private String _firstName;
        private String _lastName;
        #endregion

        #region Constructor(s)
        public Person() : base() {

            this._internal_ID = Guid.NewGuid();
            this._age = new UInt32();
            this._firstName = String.Empty;
            this._lastName = String.Empty;

            return;
        }
        #endregion

        #region Override System.Object.Equals()
```

```
public override Boolean Equals( System.Object instance ) {

    // An instance of Person or derivation
    Person _another = ( instance as Person );
    Boolean _equals = ( ( _another != null ) && ( this._internal_ID
    == _another._internal_ID ) && System.Object.ReferenceEquals
    ( this, _another ) );

    return _equals;
}

#endregion

#region Overrides System.Object.GetHashCode()
public override Int32 GetHashCode() {
    return System.HashCode.Combine<Int32>( base.GetHashCode() );
    //return base.GetHashCode();
}
#endregion

    };
};
```

.NET BCL has the `System.HashCode` .NET value type as part of the `System.Runtime.dll` .NET module/assembly that we can use for generating a hash code not based on the `System.Object.GetHashCode()` instance method.

In official documentation about .NET, Microsoft warns against certain unrecommended practices for the use of a value returned for hash codes, as shown in Figure 2-7. You will understand the importance of this warning better when we discuss implementing cloning operations later in this book.

⚠ **Warning**

It is best-practice to consider hash codes as an implementation detail, as the implementation may change across assembly versions. Do not store hash codes produced by **HashCode** in serialized structures, for example, on-disk. **HashCode** uses a statically initialized random seed to enforce this best practice, meaning that the hash codes are only deterministic within the scope of an operating system process.

Figure 2-7. *Best practices orientation about custom implementation of hash codes*

For additional information, see the official Microsoft documentation at

`https://docs.microsoft.com/en-us/dotnet/api/system.hashcode?view=net-5.0.`

You can also find additional information in the GitHub official source code for runtime fundamental libraries at

`https://github.com/dotnet/runtime/blob/master/src/libraries/System.Private.CoreLib/src/System/HashCode.cs.`

CHAPTER 3

.NET Methods: Implementation Details

This chapter covers methods that a .NET custom data type inherits from the System. Object root .NET data type and aspects of the execution environment.

Methods

Previously in this book, you read about methods that we should override for .NET custom data types. This section covers some internal aspects of inherited methods and related issues with regard to the execution environment.

About the Use of Operators

Operators are implemented as methods for implementing specific operations, and they are also implemented using the static keyword for modifier and the public keyword for access modifier (for example, when implementing the operators == and !=). Listing 3-1 shows an example of C# source code implementation, and Listing 3-2 and Listing 3-3 show the Microsoft Intermediate Language (MSIL) source code generated from a C# source code implementation, respectively:

© Roger Villela 2020
R. Villela, *Pro .NET 5 Custom Libraries*, https://doi.org/10.1007/978-1-4842-6391-4_3

Listing 3-1. C# Source Code Implementation for RVJ.Core.Person == and !=
Operators

```
                              public static Boolean operator ==( Person
                                first, Person second ) {

        return Person.ReferenceEquals( first, second );

    }

                              public static Boolean operator !=( Person
                                first, Person second ) {

        return !Person.ReferenceEquals( first, second );

    }
```

Listing 3-2. MSIL Implementation of the RVJ.Core.Business.Person.op_Equality(
RVJ.Core.Business.Person, RVJ.Core.Business.Person) Method

```
.method public hidebysig specialname static
        bool  op_Equality(class RVJ.Core.Business.Person first,
                          class RVJ.Core.Business.Person second) cil
                          managed
{
  // Code size        8 (0x8)
  .maxstack  8
  IL_0000:  ldarg.0
  IL_0001:  ldarg.1
  IL_0002:  call        bool RVJ.Core.Business.Person::ReferenceEquals
                        (object,

                                                              object)
  IL_0007:  ret
} // end of method Person::op_Equality
```

Listing 3-3. MSIL Implementation of the RVJ.Core.Business.Person.op_
Inequality(RVJ.Core.Business.Person, RVJ.Core.Business.Person) Method

```
.method public hidebysig specialname static
        bool  op_Inequality(class RVJ.Core.Business.Person first,
                            class RVJ.Core.Business.Person second) cil
                            managed
{
  // Code size        11 (0xb)
  .maxstack  8
ldarg.0
ldarg.1
call       bool RVJ.Core.Business.Person::ReferenceEquals( object,  object )
ldc.i4.0
ceq
ret
} // end of method Person::op_Inequality
```

In MSIL implementations of equality (==) and inequality (!=) operators and operations, we have the hidebysig and specialname MSIL keywords as part of the metadata.

The keyword hidebysig means "hide by signature" and is ignored by the implementation of the Virtual Execution System (VES). In ECMA-335, however, this is defined as supplied only for the use of tools such as compilers, syntax analyzers in programming languages, and code generators.

In programming language syntaxes and semantics, hidebysig defines that all declared/defined methods in a .NET custom data type *must* hide all inherited .NET methods that have a matching method signature, and this is valid for any point in the hierarchy of base class types.

When hidebysig is omitted in the metadata of the MSIL for the method, the rules in programming languages *must* hide all methods with the same name, and do not consider the signature for this scenario as a differential.

Typically, the C++ programming language follows "hide by name" as the semantics for this context, and C# and Java use both "hide by name" and "hide by signature" for semantics.

When present or not in MSIL metadata, the interpretation of this scenario for keyword `hidebysig` is part of programming language semantics, syntax, and specialized tools. At the time of this writing, the execution environment provided by VES ignores this keyword.

For the MSIL `specialname` keyword, as indicated by its name, the method needs a different and specialized treatment by specialized tools, such as compilers, metadata-validation tools, and reflection-based libraries.

This differs for the MSIL keyword `rtspecialname` (which means "runtime special name") that is applied for a metadata item when the VES-provided execution environment needs to provide a different and specialized treatment for the MSIL metadata item. This is the case with, for example, MSIL keywords `.ctor` and `.cctor` (constructor and class constructor, respectively).

Operator overloading is described through method names and setting the MSIL `specialname` bit in the metadata. This combination helps to avoid name collision between items generated by tools and the execution environment spaces versus items defined/informed through the developer's spaces.

Operator Overloading: Programming Language Semantics and Syntaxes

When operator overloading is supported by a programming language's semantics and syntaxes, and the described semantics above are also supported, the ECMA-335 specifies precise semantics for the work of operators, including the name for operator methods.

The required prefix `op_` is used as part of the name of the methods for the operators (for example, `op_Equality()` and `op_Inequality()`).

The full names of operator methods are also special and defined in ECMA-335.

The ECMA-335 specification includes an "intermediate assembly language": the MSIL. Here is a necessary distinction. When we write code using a programming language that adheres to the ECMA-335 specification, the result of the compiled code is a sequence of instructions of an MSIL instruction set. These instructions are not for real hardware or processors. Instead, they are for a virtual environment that includes some characteristics and functionalities of the elements in a real computer (exactly what the resources in the ECMA-335 specification describe).

The virtual environment specializations are based on what an advanced operating system has (for example, advanced security rules, mechanisms to constantly observe your own environment, ways to guarantee data integrity based on more flexible or disciplined rules, capacity to recognize contextuality and to be dynamically extensible and expandable, interact with different and specialized environments like data management systems, development system, other platforms and capable of host, and be hosted by other environments.

Remember that this is not a one-to-one mapping between reserved words, data structures, specialized resources, or anything else in programming languages that support the .NET platform. That is, what is formalized through the instructions in MSIL, what is defined by the ECMA-335 specification, and what is implemented by the mechanisms on the platform is what prevails.

Remember that the .NET platform is programming language, operating system, and hardware platform agnostic. So, not every operator is supported by every programming language for the platform. Consult the programming language documentation for details about supported operators.

The following list shows examples of required names for binary operators. When a compiler tool chain generates the MSIL code, the following names should be used:

- op_Addition for + symbol

- op_Subtraction for - symbol

- op_Multiply for * symbol

- op_Division for / symbol

- op_Modulus for % symbol

- op_ExclusiveOr for ^ symbol

- op_BitwiseAnd for & symbol

- op_BitwiseOr for | symbol

- op_LogicalAnd for && symbols

- op_LogicalOr for || symbols

- op_Assign for = symbol

- op_LeftShift for << symbols

- op_RightShift for >> symbols

- `op_Equality` for == symbols
- `op_GreaterThan` for > symbol
- `op_LessThan` for < symbol
- `op_Inequality` for != symbols
- `op_GreaterThanOrEqual` for >= symbols
- `op_LessThanOrEqual` for <= symbols
- `op_MemberSelection` for -> symbols
- `op_RightShiftAssignment` for >>= symbols
- `op_MultiplicationAssignment` for *= symbols
- `op_PointerToMemberSelection` for ->* symbols
- `op_SubtractionAssignment` for -= for symbols
- `op_ExclusiveOrAssignment` for ^= symbols
- `op_LeftShiftAssignment` for <<= symbols
- `op_ModulusAssignment` for %= symbols
- `op_AdditionAssignment` for += symbols
- `op_BitwiseAndAssignment` for &= symbols
- `op_BitwiseOrAssignment` for |= symbols
- `op_Comma` for , symbol
- `op_DivisionAssignment` for /= symbols

For unary operators, the names must be as follows:

- `op_Decrement`
- `op_Increment`
- `op_UnaryNegation`
- `op_UnaryPlus`
- `op_LogicalNot`
- `op_True`

- op_False

- op_AddressOf

- op_OnesComplement

- op_PointerDereference

Be aware that the .NET environment uses the full sequence for the name of a .NET type. For example, the .NET execution environment does not have the concept of namespaces. That is an element of productivity made available by tools of programming languages and with support of professional integrated development environments (IDEs), analyzers, and source code editors.

In our example, this means that the name of our sample custom .NET data type is RVJ.Core.Business.Person() and not Person() only. In fact, the set of data information used to distinguish a .NET class type has more than a sequence of names.

In the intermediate language generated, the source code is based on the elements defined in the ECMA-335 and some extensions, depending on the provider of the .NET environment implementation and features supported.

For our examples, we are using the Microsoft implementation of Common Intermediate Language (CIL), known as MSIL, but with all the features available in all supported platforms, such as Microsoft Windows, Linux distributions, and the Apple macOS.

Working with System.Object.GetType()

This section covers methods that we do not need to override in our .NET custom data types, using the System.Object.GetType() instance method as an example.

System.Object.GetType() is a noninheritable instance method defined with the public access modifier keyword, and it is nonvirtual. In that way, any instance of a .NET reference type or .NET value type can access this instance method.

Listing 3-4 shows that we have the public API for System.GetType() that is available in .NET Base Class Library (BCL).

Listing 3-4. Public API for Accessing the System.GetType() Instance Method

```
public System.Type GetType();
```

For System.Object, we have the declaration shown in Listing 3-5 for the System. Object.GetType() instance method (as-is in BCL managed source code at the time of this writing).

Listing 3-5. System.Object.GetType() Instance Method (As-Is in BCL Managed Source Code for .NET)

```
[Intrinsic]
[MethodImpl(MethodImplOptions.InternalCall]
public extern Type GetType();
```

This means that the implementation of System.Object.GetType() is provided in the C++ programming language portion of a CLR implementation, and the method is specialized, requiring an implementation provided directly by the VES in runtime, and not as ordinary C# programming language source code using a public interface of foundational BCL.

In the implementation of native portions of foundational BCL, this method does not call System.Reflection (or similar) APIs. For example, a call to the System.Object. GetType() instance method, internally calls a C++ function (method) member called ObjectNative::GetClass() that calls ObjectNative::GetClassHelper().

C++ function (method) member ObjectNative::GetClass() checks whether the type of object exists in a managed environment, as checked by the macros shown in Listing 3-6.

Listing 3-6. Verifies Whether the Type of Object Exists in the Managed Environment and Is Valid for the VES

```
#define ObjectToOBJECTREF(obj)    ((PTR_Object) (obj))
#define OBJECTREFToObject(objref) ((PTR_Object) (objref))
```

Be aware and do not confuse an unmanaged .NET type with a native .NET type, because the VES has support for both.

System.Object is a class type (and thus a reference type), a managed type, and a key piece of the foundational BCL library, framework class libraries such as the Framework Class Library (FCL), and extended/specialized libraries.

For example, we have the System.IntPtr and System.UIntPtr, which are unmanaged .NET types (and not native .NET types).

Resuming, our .NET custom data type does not need to create a new implementation for `System.Object.GetType()`.

Constructors in a .NET Data Type

A reference type always has a default constructor, which is automatically generated by the compiler of the programming language that we are using; the CLR implementation model requires this.

Listing 3-7, Listing 3-8, and Listing 3-9 show three different definitions that have the same MSIL results and semantics.

Listing 3-7. Default Constructor Generated Automatically by the Compiler, and type Implicitly Derives from the System.Object Root Type

```
namespace RVJ.Core.Business {
    public class Person {}
}
```

Listing 3-8. Default Constructor Generated Automatically by the Compiler, and type Explicitly Derives from the System.Object Root Type

```
namespace RVJ.Core.Business {
    public class Person : System.Object {}
}
```

Listing 3-9. Default Constructor Implemented by the Developer, Calls Directly the base Type in the Hierarchy, and type Explicitly Derives from the System.Object Root Type

```
namespace RVJ.Core.Business {
    public class Person : System.Object {

            public Person() : base() {} // default instance constructor.

    }
}
```

A specific MSIL keyword `rtspecialname` is applied for a metadata item when the execution environment provided by VES needs to provide a different and specialized treatment for the MSIL metadata item and respective data structures and data types. Listing 3-10 and Listing 3-11 show cases when we have MSIL keywords `.ctor` / `.cctor` (for instance, constructor and class constructor, respectively).

Listing 3-10 shows excerpts of MSIL for the `RVJ.Core.Business.Person` instance constructor of C# as shown in Listing 3-7, Listing 3-8, and Listing 3-9.

We can see that the name of the method for the instance constructor is `.ctor` and not the name of the .NET type, (`RVJ.Core.Business.Person()` in our example).

Through the MSIL source code body of an instance constructor, the default constructor of the direct .NET base type is called, also using the name `.ctor`.

The MSIL `.ctor` method means "instance constructor."

Listing 3-10. Instance Default Constructor, Uses .ctor for Identification and Uses Flag rtspecialname for Special Runtime Treatment by VES

```
.class public auto ansi beforefieldinit RVJ.Core.Business.Person
      extends [System.Runtime]System.Object {

.method public hidebysig specialname rtspecialname
        instance void  .ctor() cil managed {

  // Code size        7 (0x7)
  .maxstack  8
  ldarg.0
  call       instance void [System.Runtime]System.Object::.ctor()
  ret

} // end of method Person::.ctor

} // end of class RVJ.Core.Business.Person
```

Being a static method, the class constructor, as you can see in Listing 3-11, is using a similar pattern of instance constructors. The method for the class constructor is using `.cctor` and not the name of the .NET type (`RVJ.Core.Business.Person()` in our example).

The MSIL .cctor method means "class constructor."

Listing 3-11. The Class Constructor Is Called Before the Instance Fields Are Initialized and Instance Methods Can Be Called

```
.class public auto ansi beforefieldinit RVJ.Core.Business.Person
      extends [System.Runtime]System.Object {

.method private hidebysig specialname rtspecialname static
      void .cctor() cil managed {

  // Code size       1 (0x1)
  .maxstack  8
ret
} // end of method Person::.cctor

}
```

Constructors are important kinds of methods that we should always keep in mind for use in our .NET custom data types.

Class constructors are used by MSIL instructions for what is described in CLR jargon as "before field init" semantics.

We should override for a class that uses unmanaged resources, such as file handles or database connections that must be released when the managed object that uses them is discarded during garbage-collection automatic memory-management mechanisms.

Because the garbage collector releases managed resources automatically, we should not implement a System.Object.Finalize() method for managed objects.

In fact, the System.Object.Finalize() method does nothing by default, but we should override System.Object.Finalize() only if necessary, and only to release unmanaged resources. Reclaiming memory tends to take much longer if a finalization operation runs because such reclamation requires at least two garbage collections.

In addition, we should override the System.Object.Finalize() method for reference types only. The CLR finalizes reference types only. It ignores finalizers on value types, at least at the time of this writing.

The scope of the `System.Object.Finalize()` method is protected. We should maintain this limited scope when overriding the method in our .NET custom class type.

By keeping a `System.Object.Finalize()` instance protected method, we prevent users of our application from calling an `System.Object.Finalize()` method directly.

Every implementation of `System.Object.Finalize()` in a derived type must call its base type implementation of `System.Object.Finalize()`, and this is the only case in which application code is allowed to call `System.Object.Finalize()` directly.

An object's `Finalize` method should not call a method on any objects other than that of its base class. This is because the other objects being called could be collected at the same time as the calling object, such as in the case of a CLR shutdown.

You will learn more about constructors, VES details, and finalizers in the upcoming chapters.

CHAPTER 4

.NET Special Members: Constructors in a Managed Environment

This chapter covers special members that a .NET custom data type should implement.

Acronyms

The following acronyms are introduced in this chapter:

- Application programming interface (API)
- Code Document Object Model (CodeDOM)
- Object-oriented programming (OOP)

Special Members

Throughout these chapters, we are examining members that we should override (or not) for our .NET custom data types. At this point, we focus on internal aspects of special members (constructors and destructors, for example). This chapter focuses on constructors.

© Roger Villela 2020
R. Villela, *Pro .NET 5 Custom Libraries*, https://doi.org/10.1007/978-1-4842-6391-4_4

About Constructors in a Managed Execution Environment

For the Common Language Runtime (CLR) platform and Virtual Execution System (VES) execution environment, constructors are part of the execution model. As part of this model, they are special members of any .NET data type (reference type and value type), are implemented as methods (member functions in C++ programming language syntax, and behavior in conceptually related object-oriented programming [OOP] terminology) for the special purpose of implementing specific tasks related to initialization of the state of the data type itself and instances of the data type, via their data type member behaviors.

Being methods, constructors always have void data type as the return, and they can be implemented using the static keyword for the modifier. For the access modifier, they can use public, private, protected, or internal keywords, for example. Because of these possibilities, constructor implementation can be of two natures:

- For the .NET data type itself, in that the constructor is called in relevant literature static constructor, class constructor, or type constructor

- For an instance of the .NET data type, in that the constructor is called in relevant literature an instance constructor or a nonstatic constructor

Default Constructor

In a nonstatic definition of a .NET custom data type and on creation of an instance of such .NET data type (custom or platform provided), the "default instance constructor" is a required element for any managed data type in an instance of the CLR VES execution environment. Because of this requirement, when we use the C# programming language, for example, if we do not provide a default instance constructor explicitly, a C#/ MSIL (Microsoft Intermediate Language) tool will emit a default instance constructor automatically.

Other compilers of specific programming languages or projections that support CLR (for example, F#, C++/CLI [Common Language Infrastructure] projection, and VB.NET) also support emitting a default instance constructor implicitly. However, we always must check constructor syntax features for the specific programming languages that we are using in our projects.

Figure 4-1, Figure 4-2, Figure 4-3, and Figure 4-4 show excerpts from source code. The code is introduced in this chapter, but you will learn even more about it in Chapter 5.

These excerpts derive from sample projects available for this chapter in the folder <install_dir>\Sources\APIs\DotNET\5.0\ProCustomLibs\Ch04\RVJ.Coresolution RVJ.Core.sln, in the client console sample project and in the Buffers_Console_Client. Program.CreateType() static method in the Program.cs C# source code file.

Reflection APIs

The full source code (discussed in the next chapter and part of the sample projects) uses features and data types of .NET Base Class Library (BCL) Reflection application programming interfaces (APIs) for emitting at runtime. It uses source code in MSIL to define two new .NET custom data types: RVJ.Core.Business.Person, which derives directly from the System.Object root .NET data type from foundational BCL; and RVJ. Core.Business.Employee, which derives indirectly from System.Object of foundational BCL and directly from RVJ.Core.Business.Person.

Both .NET custom data types are emitted using .NET Reflection APIs, and each data type has a default instance constructor emitted automatically by these Reflection APIs. These same tasks are realized with the C# programming language when compiling source code, as shown in Listing 4-1.

Listing 4-1. Implementation for RVJ.Core.Business.Employee::.ctor() RVJ.Core. Business.Person::.ctor() Default Instance Constructors Generated Implicitly by C# Programming Language / MSIL Tools for Both .NET Custom Data Types

```
#region Namespaces / Assemblies
using System;
#endregion

namespace RVJ.Core.Business {

    public class Employee : RVJ.Core.Business.Person {

    // Default instance constructor emitted implicitly by C# / MSIL tools

    };

    public class Person: System.Object {
```

```
// RVJ.Core.Business.Person derived directly from System.Object root
   data type of foundational BCL

// Default instance constructor emitted implicitly by C# / MSIL tools

  };

}; // End of RVJ.Core.Business namespace(s)
```

Figure 4-1 shows the source code for a specialized instance method for definition of a default constructor, which can be a default static constructor or a default instance constructor.

We can have one parameterless constructor, which is based on the features of the Reflection APIs, also emit the sequence of MSIL instructions for the source code body of the constructor that includes the calls for the default instance constructor of the immediate base type.

In the source code excerpt shown in Figure 4-2, we are calling the System. Reflection.Emit.TypeBuilder.DefineDefaultConstructor() instance method for defining a default instance constructor, and the only argument value is a combination of flags as values of the System.Reflection.MethodAttributes enum class.

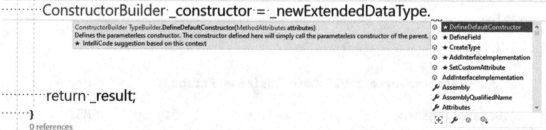

Figure 4-1. *The specialized System.Reflection.Emit.TypeBuilder. DefineDefaultConstructor() instance method in Reflection APIs that returns an instance of the System.Reflection.Emit.ConstructorBuilder .NET data type for definition of a default instance or static constructor in a data type*

```
TypeBuilder _newExtendedDataType = _moduleBuilder.DefineType("RVJ.Core.Business.Employee",
  TypeAttributes.Class | TypeAttributes.Public | TypeAttributes.Serializable |
  TypeAttributes.AutoLayout | TypeAttributes.SpecialName | TypeAttributes.UnicodeClass);

ConstructorBuilder _defaultConstructor = _newExtendedDataType.DefineDefaultConstructor
  ( MethodAttributes.Public | MethodAttributes.SpecialName | MethodAttributes.HideBySig |
  MethodAttributes.RTSpecialName | MethodAttributes.FamORAssem |
  MethodAttributes.CheckAccessOnOverride );
```

Figure 4-2. *A combination of flags for the metadata characteristics of the generated instance constructor or static constructor*

```
TypeBuilder _newExtendedDataType = _moduleBuilder.DefineType
  ("RVJ.Business.Employee", TypeAttributes.Class | TypeAttributes.Public |
  TypeAttributes.Serializable | TypeAttributes.AutoLayout |
  TypeAttributes.RTSpecialName | TypeAttributes.SpecialName |
  TypeAttributes.UnicodeClass );

ConstructorBuilder _constructor = _newExtendedDataType.DefineConstructor();
```

▲ 1 of 2 ▼ ConstructorBuilder TypeBuilder.**DefineConstructor**(**MethodAttributes attributes**, CallingConventions **callingConvention**, Type[]? **parameterTypes**)
Adds a new constructor to the type, with the given attributes and signature.
attributes: *The attributes of the constructor.*

Figure 4-3. *Another specialized instance method in the Reflection APIs of the System.Reflection.Emit.TypeBuilder .NET data type for definition of a nondefault constructor in a type, and the System.Reflection.Emit.TypeBuilder. DefineConstructor() instance method with two signatures*

```
TypeBuilder _newExtendedDataType = _moduleBuilder.DefineType("RVJ.Core.Business.Employee",
  TypeAttributes.Class | TypeAttributes.Public | TypeAttributes.Serializable |
  TypeAttributes.AutoLayout | TypeAttributes.SpecialName | TypeAttributes.UnicodeClass);


ConstructorBuilder nonDefaultConstructor = _newExtendedDataType.DefineConstructor
  ( MethodAttributes.Public | MethodAttributes.SpecialName | MethodAttributes.HideBySig |
  MethodAttributes.RTSpecialName | MethodAttributes.FamORAssem |
  MethodAttributes.CheckAccessOnOverride, CallingConventions.Standard, new Type [] { });
```

Figure 4-4. *System.Reflection.Emit.TypeBuilder.DefineConstructor(), a specialized instance method of Reflection APIs for definition of a nondefault constructor in an emitted type, and more parameters available for the metadata of the method*

Rules, Requirements, and MSIL

Rules and requirements for the default instance constructor or the default static constructor existence in the managed data type are active even for APIs of source code and metadata inspection and generation in MSIL. Examples include Reflection and CodeDOM, to cite a couple of common examples of specialized technologies in foundational libraries of BCL APIs and Framework Class Library (FCL) APIs.

Listing 4-2 shows typical C# source code for a .NET custom data type RVJ.Core. Business.Employee defined with the default instance constructor emitted implicitly by C#/MSIL tools.

Listing 4-2. Implementation for RVJ.Core.Business.Employee::.ctor() RVJ.Core. Business.Person::.ctor() Default Instance Constructors Generated Implicitly by C#/MSIL Tools for Both .NET Custom Data Types

```
#region Namespaces / Assemblies
using System;
#endregion

namespace RVJ.Core.Business {

    public class Employee : Person {

    // Default instance constructor emitted implicitly by C#/MSIL tools

    };

    public class Person: System.Object {

    // Default instance constructor emitted implicitly by C#/MSIL tools

    };

};
```

In Figure 4-5, an ILDasm.exe .NET SDK tool screen shows the content of the RVJ. Core.Business.dll assembly/module, with both RVJ.Core.Business.Employee and RVJ. Core.Business.Person .NET custom data types.

RVJ.Core.Business.Person is our .NET custom data type explicitly and is directly derived from the System.Object .NET root data type from the .NET platform fundamental BCL.

RVJ.Core.Business.Employee is our .NET custom data type that explicitly and directly derives from RVJ.Core.Business.Person, which is used here as an example for the root of our sample hierarchy of .NET custom data types.

In Figure 4-6 and Figure 4-7, an ILDasm.exe .NET SDK tool screen shows pieces of RVJ.Core.Business.Employee and RVJ.Core.Business.Person (our two .NET custom data types).

Listing 4-3 shows the MSIL automatically generated by C#/MSIL tools for RVJ.Core.Business.Employee::.ctor().

This generated MSIL, which also automatically calls the base default instance constructor for RVJ.Core.Business.Employee::.ctor(), is in this case the default instance constructor RVJ.Core.Business.Person::.ctor(), as expressed in the MSIL shown in Listing 4-3.

Listing 4-3. MSIL Implementation of the RVJ.Core.Business.Employee::.ctor() Default Instance Constructor, Also Calling the RVJ.Core.Business.Person::.ctor() Base Default Instance Constructor

```
.method public hidebysig specialname rtspecialname
        instance void  .ctor() cil managed {

  // Code size         7 (0x7)

  .maxstack  8
ldarg.0

// calling default instance constructor of base type RVJ.Core.Business.Person

call        instance void RVJ.Core.Business.Person::.ctor()

  ret

} // end of method Employee::.ctor
```

Listing 4-4 shows an excerpt with the sequence of MSIL metadata that defines the RVJ.Core.Business.Employee as an extension based on (inherited from) RVJ.Core.Business.Person. Both are .NET custom data types.

Listing 4-4. MSIL Sequence for Definition of .NET Custom Data Type RVJ.Core. Business.Employee, Which Extends the RVJ.Core.Business.Person .NET Custom Data Type

```
.class public auto ansi beforefieldinit RVJ.Core.Business.Employee extends
RVJ.Core.Business.Person {
} // end of class RVJ.Core.Business.Employee
```

Listing 4-5 and Figure 4-7 show a definition of our .NET custom data type RVJ.Core. Business.Employee with a default instance constructor implicitly emitted by C#/MSIL tools and with a static constructor of business model defined explicitly.

Note that even with the static constructor defined explicitly by a developer and the default instance constructor not defined explicitly, the C#/MSIL tools emit the sequence for a minimal .NET special method to be generated to act as the default constructor. Tasks include calls for the base default instance constructor of the base type in the hierarchy.

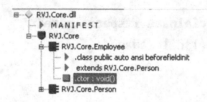

Figure 4-5. *RVJ.Core.Business.Employee default instance constructor generated by C#/MSIL tools, and the RVJ.Core.Business.Person default constructor explicitly implemented by the developer*

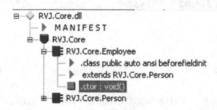

Figure 4-6. *The RVJ.Core.Business.Employee::.ctor() is declared/defined with this special name in MSIL for a default instance constructor*

Listing 4-5. Implementation for the RVJ.Core.Business.Employee::.ctor()
Default Instance Constructor Generated by C#/MSIL Tools, Even with the Static
Constructor (Class Constructor) Defined Explicitly

```
#region Namespaces/Assemblies
using System;
#endregion

namespace RVJ.Core.Business {

    public class Employee : RVJ.Core.Business.Person {

    static Employee() {  return; }

    };
};
```

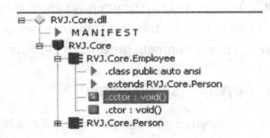

Figure 4-7. *Even with an explicitly defined static constructor RVJ.Core.Business.*
Employee::.cctor() in the provided source code programming language, the RVJ.
Core.Business.Employee::.ctor() default instance constructor is implicitly defined in
MSIL for the method acting as the default instance constructor

Metadata: MSIL Attributes in a Special Member

In MSIL implementations for a typical constructor (instance or otherwise, default or
not), the following MSIL keywords comprise part of the metadata of the method for the
constructor:

- hidebysig
- rtspecialname
- specialname

MSIL "Hide by Signature" Keyword (hidebysig)

The hidebysig MSIL keyword is ignored by the implementation of the CLR VES. In ECMA-335, however, this is defined as supplied only for the use of the specialized tools such as compilers, syntax analyzers in programming languages, and code generators.

In programming language syntax and semantics, the hidebysig keyword defines that all declared/defined methods in a .NET data type (custom or not) *must* hide all inherited .NET methods that have a matching method signature. This requirement is valid for any point in the hierarchy of base class types.

When the hidebysig keyword is omitted in the metadata of the MSIL for the method, however, programming language rules require hiding all methods with the same name (and to not consider the signature for this scenario as a differential).

Typically, the C++ programming language follows "hide by name" as the semantics in this context, and C# and Java use both "hide by name" and "hide by signature" for semantics.

When present or not in MSIL metadata, the interpretation of this scenario for the hidebysig keyword is part of the programming language semantics, syntax, and specialized tools. The execution environment provided by VES ignores this keyword.

MSIL "Special Name" Keyword (specialname)

For MSIL, the specialname keyword means that the name of method needs a different and specialized treatment by some specialized tool (for example, compilers, metadata validation tools, and Reflection-based libraries).

MSIL "Runtime Special Name" Keyword (rtspecialname)

In contrast, the MSIL rtspecialname keyword is applied for some metadata items when the execution environment provided by VES needs to provide a different and specialized treatment for the MSIL metadata item. This is the case when we have MSIL keywords .ctor and .cctor (for instance, constructor and class constructor [static constructor], respectively).

Summary

The next chapter discusses metadata and constructors in more detail and covers destructors and the CLR VES.

The sample project using Reflection APIs is used as the base from which to explore the inner workings of these elements of a .NET data type, .NET custom data type, and the management execution environment.

CHAPTER 5

Finalizer Method: The .NET Special Member

This chapter covers special members that a .NET custom data type should implement.

Special Members

Previous chapters discussed methods that we should override (or not) for our .NET custom data types. This section examines internal aspects of members that are not so "special" from a Control Language Runtime (CLR) Virtual Execution System (VES) perspective, as we have with a constructor. This chapter focuses specifically on destructors.

Special Member Destructor

Like constructors, destructors are also special members for the CLR VES and managed platform as a whole, and they are also implemented as methods in the Microsoft Intermediate Language (MSIL). However, with destructors, certain restrictions apply based on the syntax of the programming language in use (as with the C# programming language and MSIL as the intermediate language) and the semantics required by the execution environment (as with the CLR VES).

Formally, in a managed environment and CLR VES execution environment, we do not have the concept of a destructor as it exists in typical object-oriented programming (OOP) implementations. In addition, we have the direct influence of other components of the .NET platform architecture and implementation engineering (such as managed environment rules, programming language organizations and tools, and related or dependent elements).

© Roger Villela 2020
R. Villela, *Pro .NET 5 Custom Libraries*, https://doi.org/10.1007/978-1-4842-6391-4_5

When a class type or a value type is implemented, the concept of a default destructor does not apply, and no method is automatically and implicitly generated for this kind of member, as we have for constructors. Listing 5-1 and Listing 5-2 show that we can confirm this in the RVJ.Core.Business.Person and RVJ.Core.Business.Employee .NET custom data types and respective MSILs.

Listing 5-1. (Excerpt of Definition) The RVJ.Core.Business.Person Class Type Does Not Have Automatically Generated Source Code for a Destructor as We Have with a Default Constructor

```
#region Namespaces/Assemblies

using System;

#if DEBUG
using System.Diagnostics;
#endif

#endregion

namespace RVJ.Core.Business {
 public class Person : System.Object {

  #region Private fields

  private readonly Guid _internal_ID;
  private UInt32 _age;
  private String _firstName;
  private String _lastName;

  #endregion

  #region Constructor(s)
  public Person() : base() {

   this._internal_ID = Guid.NewGuid();
   this._age = new UInt32();
   this._firstName = String.Empty;
   this._lastName = String.Empty;
```

```
  return;
}

static Person() {
#if DEBUG
  Debug.WriteLine( "Class (static) constructor called.", "RVJ.Core.
  Business.Person" );
#endif

  return;
}
#endregion

#region Destructor

                        //~Person() {
//     return;
//}

#endregion
};

};
```

Listing 5-2. (Excerpt of Definition) The RVJ.Core.Business.Employee Class Type Does Not Have Automatically Generated Source Code for a Destructor as We Have with a Default Constructor

```
#region Namespaces/Assemblies

using System;

#if DEBUG
using System.Diagnostics;
#endif

#endregion

namespace RVJ.Core.Business {
```

```
public class Employee : Person {

    /*
     * Static constructor provided explicitly by the data type.
     */
    static Employee() {
        return;
    }

    // Default constructor provided explicitly by the data type
    public Employee() : base() { return; }

    #region Destructor

    //~Person() {
    //    return;
    //}

    #endregion

};
};
```

We cannot have more than one destructor, and it must be parameterless, as shown in Listing 5-1 and Listing 5-2.

Again, as shown in Listing 5-3, in MSIL we have special keywords (such as extends, public, auto and ansi) that are data type attributes that directly inform the CLR VES execution environment about what is necessary for the data types to be valid at runtime.

Listing 5-3. (Excerpt of Definition) The RVJ.Core.Business.Employee and RVJ. Core.Business.Person Class Types Have Special Keywords That Are Data Type Attributes That Are Required Metadata by CLR VES to Work Correctly with the Data Type

```
.class public auto ansi RVJ.Core.Business.Employee
        extends RVJ.Core.Business.Person {
} // end of class RVJ.Core.Business.Employee
```

```
.class public auto ansi RVJ.Core.Business.Person
       extends [System.Runtime]System.Object
{
} // end of class RVJ.Core.Business.Person
```

As shown in Listing 5-4 and Listing 5-5, for definition of methods that have the constructor role, we have MSIL special keywords, as mentioned earlier, such as public, hidebysig, special, rtspecialname, instance, cil, managed, and .ctor. These are recognized by the CLR VES execution environment for creating the total contextual representation model of the .method at runtime.

Listing 5-4. (Excerpt of Definition) The RVJ.Core.Business.Person Constructor Class Types That Made Use of Special Keywords That Are Recognized by the CLR VES for Creating the Total Contextual Representation Model at Runtime

```
.method public hidebysig specialname rtspecialname instance void  .ctor()
cil managed {
  // Code size        47 (0x2f)
  .maxstack  8
  ldarg.0
  call       instance void [System.Runtime]System.Object::.ctor()
  ldarg.0
  call       valuetype [System.Runtime]System.Guid [System.Runtime]System.
             Guid::NewGuid()
  stfld      valuetype [System.Runtime]System.Guid RVJ.Core.Business.
             Person::_internal_ID
  ldarg.0
  ldc.i4.0
  stfld      uint32 RVJ.Core.Business.Person::_age
  ldarg.0
  ldsfld     string [System.Runtime]System.String::Empty
  stfld      string RVJ.Core.Business.Person::_firstName
  ldarg.0
  ldsfld     string [System.Runtime]System.String::Empty
  stfld      string RVJ.Core.Business.Person::_lastName
  ret
} // end of method Person::.ctor
```

Listing 5-5. (Excerpt of Definition) The RVJ.Core.Business.Employee Constructor Class Types That Made Use of Special Keywords That Are Recognized by the CLR VES for Creating the Total Contextual Representation Model at Runtime

```
.method public hidebysig specialname rtspecialname  instance void  .ctor()
cil managed {
  // Code size        7 (0x7)
  .maxstack  8
ldarg.0
call        instance void RVJ.Core.Business.Person::.ctor()
ret
} // end of method Employee::.ctor
```

As shown in Figure 5-1, a destructor is an optional structural element of a managed data type, class type (reference type), and of a struct type (value type). In the MSIL, we can see that if not explicitly informed by the developer, by a feature of programming language tools for generation of source code, we have as default practice not having a method implicitly generated for acting as a destructor. That is, we have the *finalizer member*, which exhibits the opposite behavior of default practice for a default parameterless constructor.

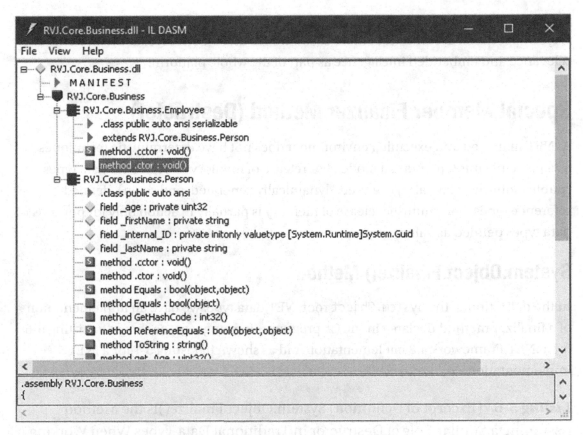

Figure 5-1. *A destructor is an optional structural element of a class type (reference type) and of a struct type (value type)*

For the CLR platform and VES execution environment, the destructor or finalizer method is a recognized piece of a managed representation and execution model. The destructor or finalizer method is a special member of any .NET data type (reference type and value type), implemented as a typical method (member functions in C++ programming language syntax and related object-oriented programming [OOP] terminology) for the special purpose of implementing specific tasks focused on resource management of the state of the data type itself and instances of the data type (but especially focused on memory management).

When we significantly rely on OOP techniques to port a base of source code, we should review our forms to see these data types. In addition, note that in a managed environment, as with the .NET platform and related components, the managed execution context of the CLR VES includes, at least, automatic memory management.

Examples of such include garbage-collector mechanisms and just-in-time compilation ways of operation at runtime. In these cases, we are at least one level above in terms of relevance and embedded intelligence as part of the whole platform.

Special Member Finalizer Method (Destructor)

A .NET managed and execution environment does not have deterministic techniques as a principle implementation model. For release of memory allocated for data types (public, internal, statically generated, dynamically generated, and so on), defined as reference types, deterministic release of memory is partially in action only for portions of data types defined as value types.

System.Object.Finalize() Method

In the definition of the `System.Object` root .NET data type, we have an implementation of a finalizer method declared in the C# programming language, as shown in Listing 5-6 for a .NET Framework 4.8 implementation and as shown in Listing 5-7 for a .NET 5 implementation.

Listing 5-6. (Excerpt of Definition) System.Object.Finalize()Is the Method Assuming a Similar Role of Destructor in Traditional Data Types When Working with OOP Techiques (For the .NET Framework 4.8, We Have This Source as the Implementation in C# Available in the object.cs Source Code File of mscorlib. csproj at `https://referencesource.microsoft.com/#mscorlib/system/ object.cs,d9262ceecc1719ab.`)

```
// Allow an object to free resources before the object is reclaimed by the GC
    //
    [ReliabilityContract(Consistency.WillNotCorruptState, Cer.Success)]
    [System.Runtime.Versioning.NonVersionable]
    ~Object()
    {
    }
```

Listing 5-7. (Excerpt of Definition) System.Object.Finalize() Is the Method
Assuming a Similar Role of Destructor in Traditional Data Types When Working
with OOP Techiques (For .NET 5, We Have This Source as the Implementation in
C# Available in the object.cs Source Code File at https://github.com/dotnet/
runtime/blob/master/src/libraries/System.Private.CoreLib/src/System/
Object.cs.)

```csharp
// Licensed to the .NET Foundation under one or more agreements.
// The .NET Foundation licenses this file to you under the MIT license.

using System.Diagnostics.CodeAnalysis;
using System.Runtime.CompilerServices;
using System.Runtime.InteropServices;
using System.Runtime.Versioning;

namespace System
{
    // The Object is the root class for all object in the CLR System. Object
    // is the super class for all other CLR objects and provide a set of
       methods and low-level
    // services to subclasses.  These services include object
       synchronization and support for clone
    // operations.
    //
    [Serializable]
    [ClassInterface(ClassInterfaceType.AutoDispatch)]
    [ComVisible(true)]
    [TypeForwardedFrom("mscorlib, Version=4.0.0.0, Culture=neutral,
    PublicKeyToken=b77a5c561934e089")]
    public partial class Object
    {
        // Creates a new instance of an Object
        [NonVersionable]
        public Object()
        {
        }
```

```
    // Allow an object to free resources before the object is reclaimed
        by the GC
    // This method's virtual slot number is hardcoded in runtimes. Do
        not add any virtual methods ahead of this.
    [NonVersionable]
    [SuppressMessage("Microsoft.Performance", "CA1821:RemoveEmpty
    Finalizers", Justification = "Base finalizer method on Object")]
    ~Object()
    {
    }
}
}
```

Microsoft official documentation defines the role of a finalizer method, the destructor, as follows:

Allows an object to try to free resources and perform other cleanup operations before it is reclaimed by garbage collection

Every time a .NET data type (custom or not, reference type or value type) has the optional destructor member, in MSIL source code generates the finalizer member (a conceptual element and a data type member), as shown in Figure 5-2 and Figure 5-3. This is as described in the ECMA-335 specification since the inception of managed and execution environments, and has been adopted by CLR VES execution environment implementation as a part of the representation model of data types for runtime operations, and as a part of the .NET platform as a whole, valid, and recognized formal element of a managed data type, as shown in Listing 5-8 and Listing 5-9.

Listing 5-8. (Excerpt of the Definition) The RVJ.Core.Business.Employee. Finalize() Method Assuming a Similar Role of a Typical Destructor

```
#region Namespaces/Assemblies

using System;

#if DEBUG
using System.Diagnostics;
#endif
```

```
#endregion

namespace RVJ.Core.Business {

    public class Employee : Person {

        /*
         * Static constructor provided explicitly by the data type.
         */
        static Employee() {
            return;
        }

        // Default constructor provided explicitly by the data type
        public Employee() : base() { return; }

// At least as of the time of this writing, we cannot have another
destructor; only one per data type is valid.

        ~Employee() {
            return;
        }

    };
};
```

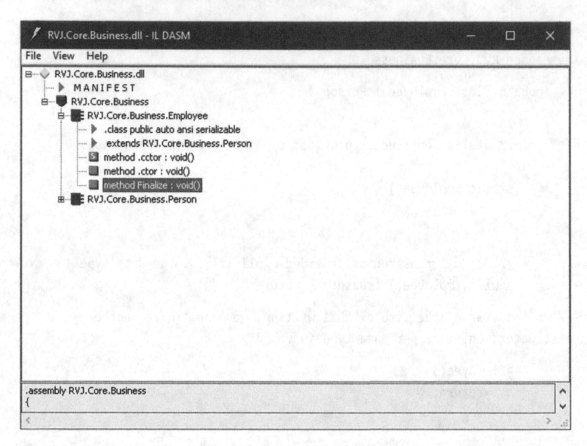

Figure 5-2. *The finalizer method in MSIL. Unlike with constructors (default or not), we have a different name, but not a special name*

```
⚡ RVJ.Core.Business.Employee::method Finalize : void()          —   □   ×
Find   Find Next
.method family hidebysig virtual instance void
        Finalize() cil managed
{
  .override [System.Runtime]System.Object::Finalize
  // Code size       10 (0xa)
  .maxstack  1
  .try
  {
    IL_0000:  leave.s     IL_0009
  } // end .try
  finally
  {
    IL_0002:  ldarg.0
    IL_0003:  call        instance void RVJ.Core.Business.Person::Finalize()
    IL_0008:  endfinally
  } // end handler
  IL_0009:  ret
} // end of method Employee::Finalize
```

Figure 5-3. *In MSIL, we have no specialname or rtspecialname MSIL keywords applied because Finalize is a common method. However, when and if used, rules apply for it to be considered valid and secure*

Listing 5-9. (Excerpt of Definition) The RVJ.Core.Business.Employee.Finalize() Method Assuming a Similar Role to a Destructor

```
.method family hidebysig virtual instance void
        Finalize() cil managed {
  .override [System.Runtime]System.Object::Finalize
  // Code size       10 (0xa)
  .maxstack  1
  .try
  {
    IL_0000:  leave.s     IL_0009
  } // end .try
  finally
  {
    IL_0002:  ldarg.0
```

```
    IL_0003:  call         instance void RVJ.Core.Business.Person::Finalize()
    IL_0008:  endfinally
  } // end handler
  IL_0009:  ret
} // end of method Employee::Finalize
```

Being methods, destructors or finalizer methods always have the void data type as the return, but they cannot be implemented using the static keyword for the modifier or the public, private, protected, internal keywords (for example) for the access modifier directly. Because of these restrictions, the following rules apply to finalizer methods:

- Have no **specialname** MSIL keyword applied because it is a common method

- Have a specific name defined to be recognized by the CLR VES as the method in the role, or similar, of a typical destructor

- Have the **hidebysig** MSIL keyword applied because it is a common method

- Have no **rtspecialname** MSIL keyword applied because it is a common method

- Are an instance member

- Are a virtual member

- Are a managed method, because we have the **cil** MSIL keyword applied in its definition

- Must override the base finalizer method of the base data type

- Are part of a chain of finalizer methods that is called based on the defined/available inheritance hierarchy of the data type family

- Have the try/catch/finally structural element, which can compromise code efficiency because of wrong use by a developer and typical code generators

The following chapter further explores the behavior of elements of special members, includes a more detailed look at constructors and the finalizer method and the .NET CLR VES, and discusses resource management (including garbage collection via interface implementations).

CHAPTER 6

.NET Manifest and Versioning for Managed Libraries

This chapter covers managed library implementation. It also discusses execution environment concepts and features that you learned about in Chapter 1 (such as assembly, module, manifest, and versioning for a managed environment).

Assemblies, Modules, Manifest, Versioning

All functionalities within a .NET executable Microsoft Intermediate Language (MSIL) are described through one or more assemblies. An assembly is a .NET entity whose purpose is to act as a deployable unit. A module is an MSIL file referenced by a logical name stored in the metadata rather than by its filename.

Common assemblies and modules that are part of the.NET Framework, .NET Core, and .NET 5 implementations include the following:

- .NET 5 assembly `System.Runtime`

  - .NET module `System.Runtime.dll`

- .NET Standard assembly `netstandard`

  - .NET module `netstandard.dll`

- .NET Core assembly `System.Runtime`

  - .NET module `System.Runtime.dll`

89

© Roger Villela 2020
R. Villela, *Pro .NET 5 Custom Libraries*, https://doi.org/10.1007/978-1-4842-6391-4_6

- .NET Framework assembly `mscorlib`

  - .NET module `mscorlib.dll`

Assembly

An assembly is a .NET entity whose purpose is to act as a deployable unit in Common Language Runtime (CLR) managed environments and with associated mechanisms, as with execution environments. Assemblies are capable of administration tasks that keep the managed environment and all resources used at runtime in an efficient and safe environment for the planned activities and related functionalities.

An assembly has different kinds of resources stored in files logically grouped for distribution, and not only executable code is stored in files associated with an assembly.

An assembly must have only *one manifest* among all its files. In addition, in the main assembly that has the entry point and will be executed rather than simply dynamically loaded, the manifest must be stored in that module.

Manifest

An assembly always has a manifest that specifies the assemblies and modules that we are using for our unit of deployment.

Listing 6-1 shows an excerpt of the manifest for the RVJ.Core.Business.dll .NET module shown in Figure 6-1.

Figure 6-1. *Manifest for the RVJ.Core.Business assembly and the RVJ.Core. Business.dll module*

Listing 6-1. Excerpt of Metadata Manifest for Assembly RVJ.Core.Business, Stored in the Module RVJ.Core.Business.dll

```
// Metadata version: v4.0.30319
.assembly extern System.Runtime {
  .publickeytoken = (B0 3F 5F 7F 11 D5 0A 3A )                    // .?_....:
  .ver 5:0:0:0
}
.assembly RVJ.Core.Business {

  .custom instance void [System.Runtime]System.Reflection.
  AssemblyFileVersionAttribute::.ctor(string) = ( 01 00 07 35 2E 30 2E 30
  2E 30 00 00 )                  // ...5.0.0.0..
  .custom instance void [System.Runtime]System.Reflection.
  AssemblyInformationalVersionAttribute::.ctor(string) = ( 01 00 07 35 2E
  30 2E 30 2E 30 00 00 )                  // ...5.0.0.0..
  .permissionset reqmin
= {[System.Runtime]System.Security.Permissions.SecurityPermissionAttribute
= {property bool 'SkipVerification' = bool(true)}}
  .hash algorithm 0x00008004

  .ver 6:0:0:0

}

.module RVJ.Core.Business.dll

// MVID: {F721CBE6-5444-4AF9-B844-9E928575E8AF}
.custom instance void [System.Runtime]System.Security.
UnverifiableCodeAttribute::.ctor() = ( 01 00 00 00 )
.imagebase 0x10000000
.file alignment 0x00000200
.stackreserve 0x00100000
.subsystem 0x0003         // WINDOWS_CUI
.corflags 0x00000001     //   ILONLY
// Image base: 0x0B6D0000
```

The directive .ver for the RVJ.Core.Business assembly has a value of 6:0:0:0, and the System.Reflection.AssemblyFileVersionAttribute attribute for the RVJ.Core. Business.dll .module has a value of 5:0:0:0. The .assembly is a directive that declares the manifest and specifies to which assembly the current module belongs. Every module *must* have one .assembly directive.

| Assembly version: | 6 | 0 | 0 | 0 |
| Assembly file version: | 5 | 0 | 0 | 0 |

Figure 6-2. *Project properties with values for "Assembly version:" assigned to the .ver directive in the manifest and the "Assembly file version" assigned to the .assembly directive in the manifest*

Listing 6-2 shows <AssemblyVersion> with a value of 6:0:0:0 assigned to the .ver directive, and the listing shows <FileVersion> with a value of 5:0:0:0 assigned to the System.Reflection.AssemblyFileVersionAttribute for .module directive.

Listing 6-2. Excerpt of Project Source Code for the Definition of the Configuration of a Project, Including .assembly and .module Versions

```
<Project Sdk="Microsoft.NET.Sdk">
  <PropertyGroup>
    <TargetFramework>net5.0</TargetFramework>
    <Authors>Roger Villela</Authors>
    <RootNamespace>RVJ.Core.Business</RootNamespace>
    <AssemblyName>RVJ.Core.Business</AssemblyName>
    <RunAnalyzersDuringBuild>false</RunAnalyzersDuringBuild>
    <FileVersion>5.0.0.0</FileVersion>
    <AssemblyVersion>6.0.0.0</AssemblyVersion>
    <Version>5.0.0.0</Version>
  </PropertyGroup>

  <PropertyGroup Condition="'$(Configuration)|$(Platform)'=='Debug|AnyCPU'">
    <DefineConstants>DEBUG;TRACE</DefineConstants>
    <AllowUnsafeBlocks>true</AllowUnsafeBlocks>
```

```
    <Optimize>true</Optimize>
    <CheckForOverflowUnderflow>true</CheckForOverflowUnderflow>
  </PropertyGroup>

</Project>
```

Module

A module is an MSIL file referenced by a logical name stored in the metadata rather than by its filename.

Listing 6-3 shows an excerpt of the syntax of the `.module` directive for RVJ.Core. Business.dll.

Listing 6-3. An Excerpt of the Syntax of the .module Directive for RVJ.Core. Business.dll, Showing the Use of Syntax and Relation for Directives .assembly, .ver, and .module

```
.assembly RVJ.Core.Business {

.ver 5:0:0:0

}

.module RVJ.Core.Business.dll
```

Listing 6-4 shows a client application named `Buffers_Console_Client` with a `.module` directive value assigned with Buffers_Console_Client.dll and with a `.assembly` directive named `Buffers_Console_Client`.

We have `.assembly extern` as the directive informing that our assembly `Buffers_ Console_Client` is referencing the assembly `RVJ.Core.Business`, and we are not informing that `.assembly RVJ.Core.Business` has a `.module` RVJ.Core.Business.dll as part of deployment unit.

This information is obtained from metadata when assemblies and modules are loaded, and the CLR Virtual Execution System (VES) and other mechanisms of a managed environment store them in internal data structs of the platform. Some are used at runtime, and others only at specific points of MSIL execution (as when metadata is checked for validation, for example).

Listing 6-4. A Client Application with .assembly Extern as the Directive
Informing That Our Assembly Buffers_Console_Client Is Referencing the
Assembly RVJ.Core.Business. We Are Not Informing That .assembly RVJ.Core.
Business Has a .module RVJ.Core.Business.dll as Part of Deployment Unit

```
.assembly extern RVJ.Core.Business {
  .ver 6:0:0:0
}

.assembly Buffers_Console_Client {

.ver 1:0:0:0

}
.module Buffers_Console_Client.dll
```

Figure 6-3 shows an example of an assembly named `Buffers_Console_Client`
stored in a module named Buffers_Console_Client.dll, and the part of MSIL of the
manifest stored in that module is shown too.

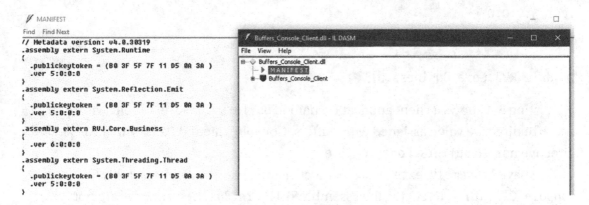

Figure 6-3. *An example of MSIL for a manifest of the assembly Buffers_Console_
Client stored in the module Buffers_Console_Client.dll*

Versioning

The version number of an assembly module is specified using the `.ver` directive. For RVJ.Core.Business, the `.assembly` directive with a value uses a sequence of four 32-bit integers in the format `Int32:Int32:Int32:Int32` (as with `6:0:0:0` for the `System.Reflection.AssemblyFileVersionAttribute` attribute for the `.module` directive with a value using `Int32:Int32:Int32:Int32`, as we have with file RVJ.Core.Business.dll with value of `5:0:0:0`).

Version numbers are captured at compile time and used as part of all references for the assemblies within each compiled module.

Some fundamental orientations are made to avoid collisions between libraries and updates.

> *Major version number*: Assemblies with the same name and with different major versions are considered not interchangeable, and the first of these 32-bit integers is considered the major version number. That major version number is used for a major rewrite of a product where backward compatibility will not be guaranteed (even by formal business contracts).
>
> *Minor version number*: Assemblies with the same name and same major version. This is the point for the use of the second of these 32-bit integers called the minor version number. It is used to indicate improvements and enhancements in each different minor version.
>
> The minor version number can also be used to indicate significant improvements, but with the intention of being backward compatible, where possible, or meaning a fully backward-compatible new version of a product.
>
> *Build version number*: At the time of this writing, we have the same software available in different hardware and operating system platforms. The third of these 32-bit integers is considered the build number and is recommended for recompilation of the same source code base for different target platforms— operating system, hardware processor, or even development tool changes or updates (for example, with integrated development environments [IDEs]).

Revision version number: The revision number is used when we
have assemblies with the same name, the same major version,
and the same minor version, but that requires a revision. The idea
of a revision is to be fully interchangeable.

This is the recommendation for the fourth of these 32-bit integers. A good example is
a security hole fix (common today) or improvements in internal algorithms.

CHAPTER 7

.NET Assemblies in a Managed Execution Environment

This chapter discusses managed libraries and covers the execution environment features that exploit publicly available managed libraries that expose a public managed view with aggregated functionalities of the fundamental data structures, data types, and behaviors internally written in the C++ programming language.

Managed Libraries

When designing and implementing .NET software libraries, .NET components, and .NET custom data types, remember that we are, in many ways, extending and aggregating in an implementation instance of the managed execution environment Common Language Runtime (CLR) Virtual Execution System (VES), which already has a flexible and productive environment with tremendous possibilities for exploring design and implementation techniques for software development.

The CLR Common Language Infrastructure (CLI) specifies a foundational library called the Base Class Library (BCL), with components and functionalities written in C# and C++ programming languages.

The .NET BCL foundational library has data types, components, functionalities, and also fundamental types (some built in, others not).

© Roger Villela 2020
R. Villela, *Pro .NET 5 Custom Libraries*, https://doi.org/10.1007/978-1-4842-6391-4_7

Data Types, Components, and Functionalities

.NET data types, .NET components, and .NET functionalities are all stored physically in .NET modules. We know these as binary files with stored executable code, as we have with .EXE and .DLL files in the Microsoft Windows operating system.

These .NET modules are versioned physically, grouped logically for distribution, and deployed as a logical unit using the .NET entity defined as a .NET assembly, which can also be versioned independently of the .NET module per se, as shown in Chapter 6. Note that a .NET module, which is a typical physical file, can be logically associated with different .NET assemblies, as we have with a .DLL with shared functionalities created to be used independently of the target application and even of other libraries.

As explained in Chapter 6, the following are examples of common assemblies and modules that are part of .NET Framework, .NET Core, and .NET 5 implementations:

- .NET 5 assembly `System.Runtime`

  - Module `System.Runtime.dll`

- .NET Standard assembly `netstandard`

  - Module `netstandard.dll`

- .NET Core assembly `System.Runtime`

  - Module `System.Runtime.dll`

- .NET Framework assembly `mscorlib`

  - Module `mscorlib.dll`

Listing 7-1 shows that the Microsoft Intermediate Language (MSIL) manifest of sample file RVJ.Core.Business.dll has a `.ver` attribute for RVJ.Core.Business `.assembly` with a value of 1:1:1:1 and a `System.Reflection.AssemblyFileVersionAttribute` attribute for RVJ.Core.Business.dll `.module` with a value of 2:2:2:2.

Listing 7-1. Assembly and Module Attributes for Versions Are Independent in .NET Mechanisms

```
.assembly extern System.Runtime
{
  .publickeytoken = (B0 3F 5F 7F 11 D5 0A 3A )                    // .?_....:
  .ver 5:0:0:0
}
.assembly RVJ.Core.Business
{
  .custom instance void [System.Runtime]System.Runtime.CompilerServices.
  CompilationRelaxationsAttribute::.ctor(int32) = ( 01 00 08 00 00 00 00 00 )
  .custom instance void [System.Runtime]System.Runtime.CompilerServices.
  RuntimeCompatibilityAttribute::.ctor() = ( 01 00 01 00 54 02 16 57 72 61
  70 4E 6F 6E 45 78   // ....T..WrapNonEx
       63 65 70 74 69 6F 6E 54 68 72 6F 77 73 01 )        // ceptionThrows.

  // --- The following custom attribute is added automatically, do not
         uncomment -------
  //  custom instance void [System.Runtime]System.Diagnostics.Debuggable
      Attribute::.ctor(valuetype [System.Runtime]System.Diagnostics.
      DebuggableAttribute/DebuggingModes) = ( 01 00 02 00 00 00 00 00 )

  .custom instance void [System.Runtime]System.Runtime.Versioning.
  TargetFrameworkAttribute::.ctor(string) = ( 01 00 18 2E 4E 45 54 43 6F 72
  65 41 70 70 2C 56   // ....NETCoreApp,V
      65 72 73 69 6F 6E 3D 76 35 2E 30 01 00 54 0E 14   // ersion=v5.0..T..
      46 72 61 6D 65 77 6F 72 6B 44 69 73 70 6C 61 79   // FrameworkDisplay
      4E 61 6D 65 00 )                                   // Name.
  .custom instance void [System.Runtime]System.Reflection.
  AssemblyCompanyAttribute::.ctor(string) = ( 01 00 0D 52 6F 67 65 72 20 56
  69 6C 6C 65 6C 61   // ...Roger Villela
                                                    00 00 )

  .custom instance void [System.Runtime]System.Reflection.
  AssemblyConfigurationAttribute::.ctor(string) = ( 01 00 05 44 65 62 75 67
  00 00 )                      // ...Debug..
```

```
.custom instance void [System.Runtime]System.Reflection.
AssemblyFileVersionAttribute::.ctor(string) = ( 01 00 07 32 2E 32 2E 32
2E 32 00 00 )                   // ...2.2.2.2..
.custom instance void [System.Runtime]System.Reflection.
AssemblyInformationalVersionAttribute::.ctor(string) = ( 01 00 07 31 2E
30 2E 30 2E 30 00 00 )                // ...1.0.0.0..
.custom instance void [System.Runtime]System.Reflection.
AssemblyProductAttribute::.ctor(string) = ( 01 00 11 52 56 4A 2E 43 6F 72
65 2E 42 75 73 69   // ...RVJ.Core.Busi
              6E 65 73 73 00 00 )                          // ness..
.custom instance void [System.Runtime]System.Reflection.
AssemblyTitleAttribute::.ctor(string) = ( 01 00 11 52 56 4A 2E 43 6F 72
65 2E 42 75 73 69   // ...RVJ.Core.Busi
              6E 65 73 73 00 00 )                          // ness..
.permissionset reqmin
          = {[System.Runtime]System.Security.Permissions.Security
            PermissionAttribute = {property bool 'SkipVerification'
            = bool(true)}}
.hash algorithm 0x00008004
.ver 1:1:1:1
}
.module RVJ.Core.Business.dll
// MVID: {16B05BC4-28BD-4BE2-844C-BF5FFF9F4C9D}
.custom instance void [System.Runtime]System.Security.
UnverifiableCodeAttribute::.ctor() = ( 01 00 00 00 )
.imagebase 0x10000000
.file alignment 0x00000200
.stackreserve 0x00100000
.subsystem 0x0003        // WINDOWS_CUI
.corflags 0x00000001     //  ILONLY
// Image base: 0x068F0000
```

Figures 7-1 and 7-2, respectively, show examples of setting the .ver attribute for the .assembly directive and the System.Reflection.AssemblyFileVersionAttribute attribute for the RVJ.Core.Business.dll .module, and the effect on operating system–recognized properties (attributes) of objects, as we have with files.

Figure 7-1 shows a Microsoft Visual Studio window for project properties with the Assembly version field having a value of 1:1:1:1 and the Assembly file version field having a value of 2:2:2:2.

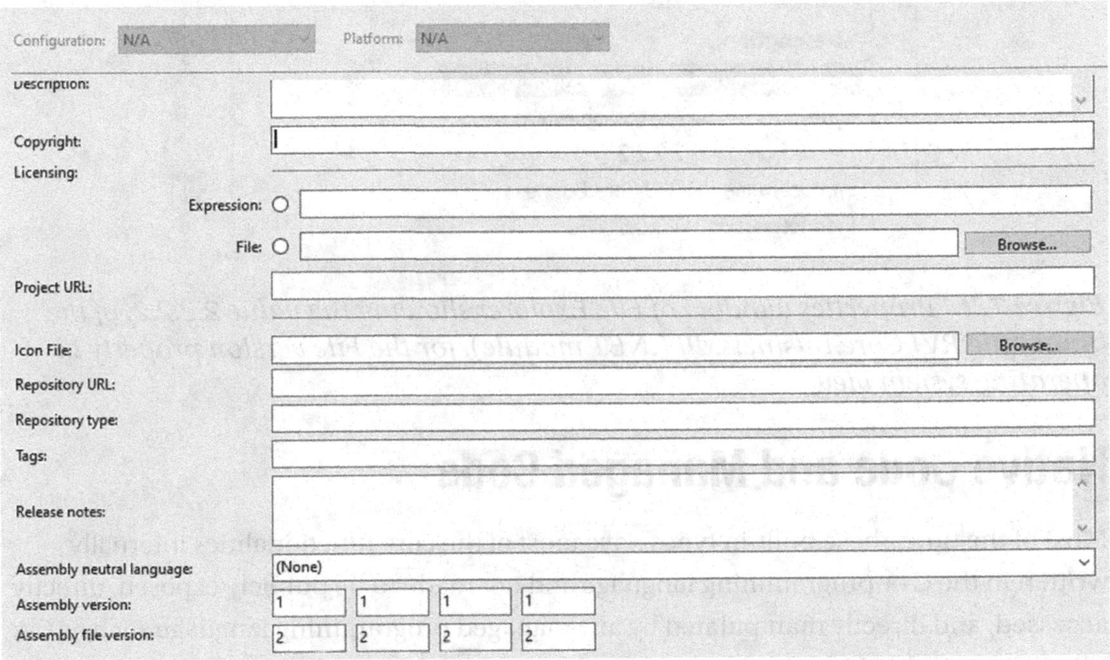

Figure 7-1. *Project properties with the Assembly version field with a value of 1:1:1:1 and the Assembly file version field with a value of 2:2:2:2*

Figure 7-2 shows the File Explorer Properties window of the file RVJ.Core.Business. dll (.NET module) showing a value of 2:2:2:2.

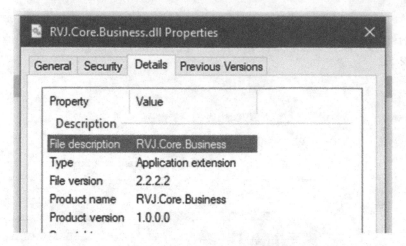

Figure 7-2. *Properties window of File Explorer showing the value 2.2.2.2, of the binary file RVJ.Core.Business.dll (.NET module), for the File version property in operating system view*

Native Code and Managed Code

Most of the time, these built-in types have most of the core functionalities internally written in the C++ programming language and not made to be publicly exposed, directly accessed, and directly manipulated by any managed programming language such as C#, VB.NET, F#, C++/CLI projection, or any other programming language or projection. In addition, they are specified by the CLR Common Type System (CTS), implemented and supported directly within the CLR VES, both part of the CLR CLI.

Listing 7-2 shows an excerpt of ArrayNative.cpp of .NET 5 available at https://github.com/dotnet/runtime/blob/master/src/coreclr/src/classlibnative/bcltype/arraynative.cpp.

Listing 7-2. Excerpt of the ArrayNative.cpp Source Code, Part of the C++ of System.Array Managed Data Type, .NET 5

```
// Licensed to the .NET Foundation under one or more agreements
// The .NET Foundation licenses this file to you under the MIT license.
//
// File: ArrayNative.cpp
//

//
```

```
// This file contains the native methods that support the Array class.
//

#include "common.h"
#include "arraynative.h"
#include "excep.h"
#include "field.h"
#include "invokeutil.h"

#include "arraynative.inl"

FCIMPL1(void, ArrayNative::Initialize, ArrayBase* array)
{
  FCALL_CONTRACT;

  if (array == NULL)
  {
    FCThrowVoid(kNullReferenceException);
  }

  MethodTable* pArrayMT = array->GetMethodTable();

  TypeHandle thElem = pArrayMT->GetArrayElementTypeHandle();
  if (thElem.IsTypeDesc())
    return;

  MethodTable * pElemMT = thElem.AsMethodTable();
  if (!pElemMT->HasDefaultConstructor() || !pElemMT->IsValueType())
    return;

  ARRAYBASEREF arrayRef (array);
  HELPER_METHOD_FRAME_BEGIN_1(arrayRef);

  ArrayInitializeWorker(&arrayRef, pArrayMT, pElemMT);

  HELPER_METHOD_FRAME_END();
}
FCIMPLEND
```

Listing 7-3 shows an excerpt of ArrayNative.h of .NET 5 available at https://github. com/dotnet/runtime/blob/master/src/coreclr/src/classlibnative/bcltype/ arraynative.h.

Listing 7-3. Excerpt of ArrayNative.h Source Code, Part of a C++ System.Array Managed Data Type, .NET 5

```
// Licensed to the .NET Foundation under one or more agreements
// The .NET Foundation licenses this file to you under the MIT license
//
// File: ArrayNative.h
//

//
// ArrayNative
// This file defines the native methods for the array.
//

#ifndef _ARRAYNATIVE_H_
#define _ARRAYNATIVE_H_

#include "fcall.h"

class ArrayNative {
public:

  static FCDECL1(INT32, GetCorElementTypeOfElementType, ArrayBase*
  arrayUNSAFE);

  static FCDECL1(void, Initialize, ArrayBase* pArray);

  static FCDECL2(FC_BOOL_RET, IsSimpleCopy, ArrayBase* pSrc, ArrayBase* pDst);

  static FCDECL5(void, CopySlow, ArrayBase* pSrc, INT32 iSrcIndex,
  ArrayBase* pDst, INT32 iDstIndex, INT32 iLength);

  // This method will create a new array of type type, with zero lower
  // bounds and rank.
  static FCDECL4(Object*, CreateInstance, void* elementTypeHandle, INT32
  rank, INT32* pLengths, INT32* pBounds);
```

```
// This method will return a TypedReference to the array element.
static FCDECL4(void, GetReference, ArrayBase* refThisUNSAFE, TypedByRef*
elemRef, INT32 rank, INT32* pIndices);

// This set of methods will set a value in an array.
static FCDECL2(void, SetValue, TypedByRef* target, Object* objUNSAFE);

// This method will initialize an array from a TypeHandle
// to a field.
static FCDECL2_IV(void, InitializeArray, ArrayBase* vArrayRef,
FCALLRuntimeFieldHandle structField);

private:
// Helper for CreateInstance
static void CheckElementType(TypeHandle elementType);

// Return values for CanAssignArrayType
enum AssignArrayEnum
{
  AssignWrongType,
  AssignMustCast,
  AssignBoxValueClassOrPrimitive,
  AssignUnboxValueClass,
  AssignPrimitiveWiden,
};

// The following functions are all helpers for ArrayCopy.
static AssignArrayEnum CanAssignArrayType(const BASEARRAYREF pSrc, const
BASEARRAYREF pDest);

static void CastCheckEachElement(BASEARRAYREF pSrc, unsigned int srcIndex,
BASEARRAYREF pDest, unsigned int destIndex, unsigned int length);

static void BoxEachElement(BASEARRAYREF pSrc, unsigned int srcIndex,
BASEARRAYREF pDest, unsigned int destIndex, unsigned int length);

static void UnBoxEachElement(BASEARRAYREF pSrc, unsigned int srcIndex,
BASEARRAYREF pDest, unsigned int destIndex, unsigned int length);
```

```
static void PrimitiveWiden(BASEARRAYREF pSrc, unsigned int srcIndex,
BASEARRAYREF pDest, unsigned int destIndex, unsigned int length);
```

```
};
```

```
#endif // _ARRAYNATIVE_H_
```

Figure 7-3 and Figure 7-4 show some comments related to documentation of ArrayNative.cpp C++ source code with implementation (definition) of members of the ArrayNative C++ class, and an ArrayNative.h C++ header file, with the declaration of ArrayNative class members in the C++ programming language.

Be aware that these pieces of source code are specialized implementations of critical CLR data types that run exclusively inside the execution engine environment (VES).

These same architectural components and implementation engineering are adopted for native parts of other fundamental and critical .NET managed data types, such as System.String and System.Object (the root of every .NET data type). As indicated, the VES handles much of the work, and we have more interesting functionalities within this mechanism.

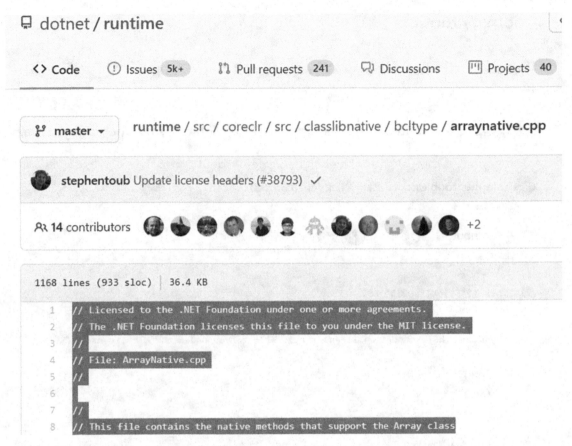

Figure 7-3. Excerpt of ArrayNative.cpp comments in source code for implementation documentation in the C++ programming language of functionalities of the System.Array managed class type

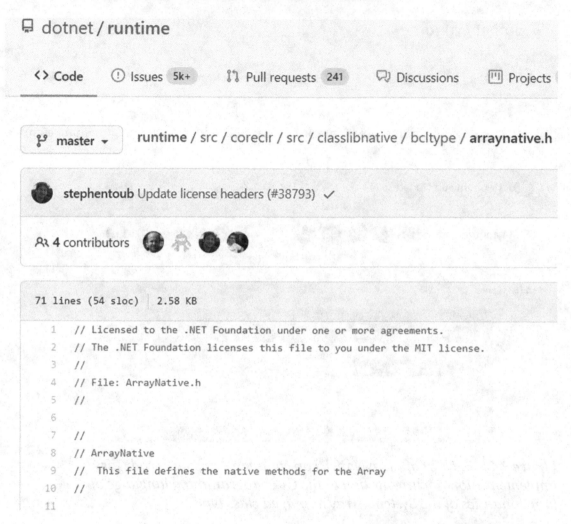

Figure 7-4. Excerpt of ArrayNative.h comments in a header file for documentation of declarations in the C++ programming language of members and functionalities of the ArrayNative C++ class

If we look at implementations of the foundational .NET BCL and more complete .NET FCL libraries, we will find that the infrastructure of various pieces is made with the C++ programming language, in many cases not even using advanced capabilities of object-oriented programming (OOP), using the procedural programming capabilities encapsulated with an OOP-based visualization for organization of the data structures and access to them.

We should ignore technologies like Microsoft Visual C++, the C++ programming language, C++/CLI, CIL, and the Assembly programming language available for development and think that we should find some solution via a block of code written only in the C# programming language; doing so would be unreasonable.

Despite this, managed programming languages such as C#, F#, VB.NET, C++/CLI projection, and others can access these built-in types and their functionalities and can create .NET software components and .NET software libraries using them.

Formally, in a managed environment and CLR VES execution environment, we do not envision a physical computer. Instead, we anticipate a virtual computer that supports through its capabilities, features as we've seen in typical OOP implementations and we have direct influence of other components of .NET platform architecture and implementation engineering, in managed environment rules, programming languages organizations and tools, and related or dependent elements.

When we are porting a base of source code largely based on OOP techniques, we should review our forms to check these data types. We also need to understand that in a managed environment (as we have with the .NET platform and their components) the managed execution context of the CLR VES includes, at least, automatic memory management, as we have with garbage collector mechanisms and just-in-time compilation operation at runtime. We are at least one level above in terms of relevance and embedded intelligence as part of the whole platform.

When designing a library, we are envisioning software that can be used over a reasonable commercial period and in a number of target environments (as with the .NET platform).

Duplicating the code base is complicated and undesirable, even with simple .NET class libraries, and trying to create code bases with many shortcuts is of dubious merit.

When .NET libraries use a managed programming language, as we have with the C# programming language, and declare a variable of `System.String`, or when C++/CLI declares a handle to the object for the type `System.String`, both are doing the same thing. That is, they are syntactically describing a script for the compilers that generate the metadata using the data structures and data types described in the CLI by the CTS, formalized by the metadata system defined by the CLI, and consumed (executed <==> managed) by the mechanisms that are part of the VES.

To facilitate these tasks for compilation tools, specialized code generators, integrated development environment (IDE)-based products, and command-line tools (to name just a few examples), a foundational and extensible library is critical.

Based on the fundamental types specified by the CTS, formalized by metadata systems, and implemented and managed via VES mechanisms, it is possible to create more specialized managed libraries covering broader contexts, having .NET BCL and Framework Class Library (FCL) as starting points. As you will remember, the .NET platform comprises CLR, BCL, FCL, and a set of specialized components and tools.

Specialized technologies designed and implemented with a mix of managed code and C++ programming language that target Microsoft Windows platform are not portable.

A subset of .NET Framework technologies (that is, a subset of the CLR functionalities, a subset of BCL) was chosen to create the .NET Core, and based on .NET Core, ASP.NET Core was created.

We now have .NET 5, .NET 6 (Long Term Support [LTS] release scheduled for November 2021), and more included as part of this technological and also political initiative that are porting elements of .NET technologies for other platforms (hardware and software) such as Qualcomm ARM, Unix-based implementation such as BSD-based operating system such as FreeBSD, Apple products, and NetBSD, and non-BSD UNIX such as Linux implementations and RedHat Enterprise, for example.

This list is incomplete, so check the Microsoft sites and Microsoft Git repositories for more comprehensive information about these initiatives.

As of this writing, GitHub has provided anticipated release dates at `https://github.com/dotnet/core/blob/master/roadmap.md` and milestone information at `https://github.com/dotnet/runtime/milestones`, respectively, as shown in Figure 7-5 and Figure 7-6.

Upcoming Ship Dates

Milestone	Release Date
.NET Core 2.1.x (servicing)	LTS (Long Term Support) release. Approximately every 1-2 months or as needed.
.NET Core 3.1.x (servicing)	LTS (Long Term Support) release. Approximately every 1-2 months or as needed.
.NET 5.0	Release scheduled for November 2020
.NET 6.0	LTS (Long Term Support) release, scheduled for November 2021
.NET 7.0	Release scheduled for November 2022
.NET 8.0	LTS (Long Term Support) release, scheduled for November 2023

Figure 7-5. *Table from GitHub for upcoming ship dates of the newly announced versions of .NET multiplatform*

Figure 7-6. *Information from the milestones page for the .NET versions 5 and 6*

Index

A

Application programming
interfaces (APIs)
HeapAlloc() function, 12
reflection, 65–67

B

Base Class Library (BCL)
architectural infrastructure, 3
CTS System.Object, 17
fundamental types, 9–10, 97
reflection APIs, 65
System.GetType(), 57–58
System.Object reference type, 31–33, 37

C

Common Intermediate Language (CIL), 4
Common Language Infrastructure (CLI), 2
Common Language Runtime (CLR)
assembly, 90
constructors, 64
contextual resources, 18
data types, 29
destructors, 75
environment and technologies, 8, 11
execution environment, 31
managed libraries, 97
native code, 102

Common Language Specification (CLS), 3
Common Type System (CTS), 3
contextualized type, 13
contextual resources, 18
fundamental built-in data
types, 13–14
hardware platform, 14–16
supports types, 16–18
System.Object reference type, 17
variable declaration, 17
Components, 98–102
Constructors, 59–62
execution environment, 64
implementation, 64
metadata/MSIL attributes
hidebysig MSIL keyword, 72
methods, 71
rtspecialname keyword, 72
specialname keyword, 72
MSIL tools/implementation, 64, 69
projections, 64
reflection APIs
instance/static data types, 66
meaning, 65
metadata characteristics, 67
parameters, 67
source code, 65
specialized instance method, 67
rules/requirements, 68–71
RVJ.Core.Business.Employee, 70–71

113

© Roger Villela 2020
R. Villela, *Pro .NET 5 Custom Libraries*, https://doi.org/10.1007/978-1-4842-6391-4

D

Data types
  execution environment, 98
  inheritance model, 37
  methods (*see* System.Object.Equals()
      method)
  planning/implementation, 29
  reference types/value types
    attributes, 34–35
    concrete classes, 32
    contextual comprehension, 30
    FCL libraries, 33
    interface type, 30–31
    root type, 29
    System.Array/System.String, 34
    System.Object, 31
  System.Object.GetHashCode(), 46–49
  value type, 35–38
Destructors
  class type source code, 76–79
  CLR VES, 75
  contextual representation model, 80
  data type attributes, 78
  execution environment, 75
  structural element, 81

E

ECMA-335 standard specification
  abstract data type, 6
  architectural infrastructure, 3, 4
  CLI (*see* Common Language
      Infrastructure (CLI))
  definition, 2
  entry-point member method, 7
  intermediate assembly language, 4

  MSIL source code, 7
  programming language, 5
  reference type, 6
  System.Object root data type, 5
  web page information, 2
Execution environment, 97
  data types/components/functionalities
    assembly and module
      attributes, 99–101
    binary files, 98
    implementations, 98
    modules, 98
    properties window, 102–103
  native/manage code, 102
    ArrayNative.cpp source code,
      102–104
    ArrayNative.h source
      code, 104–106
    command-line tools, 109
    GitHub table, 110
    header file, 108
    libraries, 109
    milestones page, 111
    System.Array managed
      class type, 107
    virtual computer, 109

F, G, H

Finalizer method, *see* Destructors
Framework Class Library (FCL), 33, 110
Functionalities, 98

I, J, K

Intermediate Language Disassembler
    (ILDASM) tool, 23–24

L

Libraries
    assemblies, 90
    implementations, 89–90
    manifest, 90–93
    module, 93–94
    versioning, 95–96
Long Term Support (LTS), 110

M

Managed libraries, 97
Manifest development
    assemblies/module, 90
    project properties, 92
    RVJ.Core.Business.dll module, 91
    source code, 92–93
Members, *see* Constructors
Metadata, 3
Methods
    constructor, 59–62
    operations, 51–54
    operator overloading, 54–57
    System.Object.GetType(), 57–59
Microsoft Intermediate
        Language (MSIL), 5, 89, 98
Module, 93–94

N

.NET platform
    attributes, 11
    CLR environment/technologies, 8
    ECMA-335 (*see* ECMA-335 standard
        specification)
    GitHub, 8
    HeapAlloc() function, 12
    implementation attributes, 11
    managed environment, 9
    pinvokeimpl method, 12
    programming languages, 9
    string reference type, 9
    types defined, 9, 10
    unified type system, 9
    unmanaged code, 11–12
    virtual computer, 8

O, P, Q, R

Object-oriented programming (OOP), 108
Operations
    hidebysig keywords, 53
    MSIL implementation, 52–53
    rtspecialname keyword, 54
    source code implementation, 51
    specialname keyword, 54
Operator overloading
    binary operators, 55–57
    intermediate assembly language, 54
    programming languages, 55
    semantics/syntaxes, 54
    virtual environment, 55

S, T, U

Semantics, 4, 54
System.Object.Equals() method
    access modifier keyword, 39–40
    equality (==) and inequality (!=)
        operators, 46–47
    expressions, 43–45
    implementation, 41
    instance method, 39
    specialized implementation, 42–44

System.Object.Finalize() method
  finalizer method, 84
  managed data type, 84
  MSIL, 86
  OOP techniques, 83
  rules/restrictions, 88
  RVJ.Core.Business.Employee.Finalize()
    method, 87
  specialname/rtspecialname, 87
  traditional data types, 82
System.Object.GetHashCode()
    method, 46–49
System.Object.GetType() method, 57–59
System.Reflection.Emit.TypeBuilder.
    DefineDefaultConstructor()
    method, 66

V, W, X, Y, Z

Virtual execution system (VES)
  assemblies, 20
  CLI PE/COFF module, 19
  destructors, 75
  dynamic assemblies, 21
  element organization, 22–23
  entry point method, 24–27
  fundamental keywords, 26
  fundamental types, 18
  ISLASM tool, 23–24
  modules, 19–22, 93
  single-file static
      assembly, 23
  static assemblies, 20

Printed in the United States
By Bookmasters